# 100

## THINGS TO DO IN PUERTO RICO BEFORE YOU DIE

To SARA + PAUL,

Come Visit PR!

Crash Boat Beach
(Photo credit: Victor M. Velázquez / Evo Photography)

# 100 THINGS TO DO IN PUERTO RICO BEFORE YOU DIE

AMY GORDON

Reedy Press
PO Box 5131
St. Louis, MO 63139, USA
www.reedypress.com



Library of Congress Control Number: 2019936702

ISBN: 9781681062143

Design by Jill Halpin

Printed in the United States of America
19 20 21 22 23   5 4 3 2 1

Please note that websites, phone numbers, addresses, and company names are subject to change or cancellation. We did our best to relay the most accurate information available, but due to circumstances beyond our control, please do not hold us liable for misinformation. When exploring new destinations, please do your homework before you go.

# DEDICATION

To the people of Puerto Rico, the heart and soul of these beautiful islands.

• • • • • • • • • • • • • • • • • • • • • • • • • •

Museo de Arte de Puerto Rico
(Photo Credit: Amy Gordon)

# CONTENTS

**Music and Entertainment**



**Sports and Recreation**

**Culture and History**

A Game of Dominoes
(Photo Credit: Elliott Anderson)

# PREFACE

*Bienvenidos a Puerto Rico!* Get ready to embark on an extraordinary adventure—no passport required. Puerto Rico is an incredible place packed with beaches and mountains, forests and farmland, modern cities, and rustic paradises. Researching and writing this book was an enlightening process, but whittling down more than 3,500 square miles to just one hundred items was tough. My goal was to highlight the best of the best, but I encourage you to use these pages as a guide rather than a checklist. If you're inspired to visit a place you've never been, spend some time there. Eat in the restaurants, talk to the locals, stay the night. Who knows what wonders you'll discover for yourself?

Puerto Rico's complicated history has given rise to a vibrant culture of anachronisms. It is part of the United States but also its own country. It has two national languages: Spanish and English. It's an archipelago of three inhabited islands—one of which is named Puerto Rico—and dozens of cays. Throughout this book, when I refer to "the island," I am almost always talking about the main island of Puerto Rico. When you see "the islands," I'm including Vieques and Culebra, which are accessible by air or sea.

When I first visited Puerto Rico, I found a piece of my heart that I hadn't known was missing. I am honored to share it with you.

Chocobar Cortés
(Photo Credit: Daniela Romero @supakid)

# ACKNOWLEDGMENTS

This book would not have been possible without the help of so many people. Jilly, Jacob, and Matthew, for their endless supply of love and support. The Vieques Peeps who were so generous with their time and expertise, especially Yanira, Jose, Carlos, Mike, Giancarlo, Carlito, Dave, Heather, Thomas, Tom, Tyler, Kate, John, and Sara. My sister Katie Kelley. My rocks Kim, Jodi, Grobie, Rachel, Andi, Scott, Mara, Maria, Joan, Fish, Katie, Jessie, and Gina. Carlos Rodriguez, Ginnette Montes, and the team at Vieques Air Link. The staff at all of the attractions and municipalities I visited. Irene Levy Baker. The team at Reedy Press. All of the photographers who contributed their work. The geniuses behind Google Maps. And the countless people I met along the way who were so excited about this project and eager to offer advice, from the scientists in Arecibo to the musicians in San Germán to the skinny dippers in Manatí.

Tropical Fruits at the San Sebastián Market
(Photo Credit: Amy Gordon)

# FOOD AND DRINK

1

# SAVOR EVERY BITE
## OF A FIVE-STAR MEAL IN SAN JUAN

Sometimes a meal is more than just a meal; it's an experience that leaves you wondering just how the geniuses in the kitchen could have created such a masterpiece. In Puerto Rico's capital city, a group of visionary chefs have catapulted the island into the realm of gastronomic greatness. At Marmalade in Old San Juan, Chef Peter Schintler's meticulous dishes are like poetry on a plate. Over in Santurce, the aesthetic allure of the creative menu at Santaella is rivaled only by the chic style of the fashion-forward clientele. Chef Jose Enrique allows the island's seasonal bounty to dictate the curated menu at his eponymous eatery, and in Condado, Chef Mario Pagán's progressive cooking techniques make you feel like you're tasting ingredients for the first time, no matter how many times you've tried them before.

**TIP**

Reservations can be hard to come by at these fine-dining outposts, but they all offer first-come, first-served seating at the bar.

**Marmalade Restaurant & Wine Bar**
317 Calle Fortaleza, Old San Juan
787-724-3969
marmaladepr.com

**Santaella**
219 Calle Canals, Santurce
787-725-1611
josesantaella.com

**Jose Enrique**
176 Calle Duffaut, Santurce
787-725-3518
joseenriquepr.com

**Mario Pagán**
1110 Ave. Magdalena, Condado
787-522-6444
mariopaganrest.com

2

# TAKE A WATER TAXI TO LUNCH

## AT LAGO DOS BOCAS

Sandwiched between Utuado and Arecibo, Lago Dos Bocas is a glass-like lake surrounded by towering trees and elegant homes. This serene setting offers the perfect backdrop for a leisurely lunch at Paisaje Escondido Restaurante, a charming family eatery that's only accessible by boat. To reach the restaurant, board a water taxi and settle in for a twelve-minute ride to the open-air restaurant, where you're likely to dine amidst multigenerational families spending the day together, couples holding hands over a romantic meal, and savvy tourists seeking out this hidden gem. The menu features freshly prepared, home-style Puerto Rican food, with options like pork chops, tostones, churrasco, and mofongo stuffed with lobster, alongside natural tropical fruit juices and frozen cocktails. Paisaje Escondido Restaurante is open for lunch on Saturdays and Sundays.

Lago Dos Bocas Pier, PR-123, Arecibo

Paisaje Escondido Restaurante, 787-473-8250
facebook.com/lacasadeltrifongo

**TIP**

The boat ride is free for restaurant customers, but bring cash to tip your captain.

3

# PICK YOUR OWN STRAWBERRIES
## AT SWEETWATER FARM

Sweetwater Farm is on a mission to revive Puerto Rico's agricultural roots—and plant some new ones. After honing his horticultural skills in Florida, José Torres opened Sweetwater in his hometown of Barranquitas in 2016. The innovative farm cultivates five varieties of strawberries, a novelty among locally grown fruits. Show up on Saturday to pick your own berries right off the vine and bite into them while they're still warm from the sun. Through vertical hydroponics, Sweetwater can grow as many as twenty plants in just one square foot of space. In addition to berries, the sixteen-acre farm harvests more than twenty-five types of organically grown produce, including beets, scallions, kale, and several types of lettuce, which it sells to some of the island's top restaurants.

Carr. 779 km 8.9, Bo. Quebradillas, Barranquitas
787-399-3614
facebook.com/swfarmpr

### TIP

While the pick-your-own experience is only offered one day a week, you can purchase the farm's fresh fruits and vegetables at the on-site market Tuesday through Saturday.

4

# DRINK A PIÑA COLADA
## IN THE CITY WHERE IT WAS BORN

If you've ever gotten drunk from a piña colada, you have Puerto Rico to thank. This deliciously boozy frozen cocktail was born right here in San Juan, but exactly where, when, and by whom is a topic of heated debate. The Caribe Hilton in Condado attests that Ramón "Monchito" Marrero first created the frosty mixture of pineapple, coconut, and rum while tending bar at the hotel in 1954, but Barrachina in Old San Juan also takes the credit, declaring that its own bartender, Ramón Portas Mingot, invented it in 1963. Choosing which story to believe is up to you, but the best (and most fun) way to make a fair ruling on Puerto Rico's national drink is to sample them both. After all, one umbrella-laden tropical cocktail is never enough.

Caribe Hilton
1 Calle San Gerónimo, Condado
787-721-0303
caribehilton.com

Barrachina
104 Calle Fortaleza, Old San Juan
787-725-7912
barrachina.com

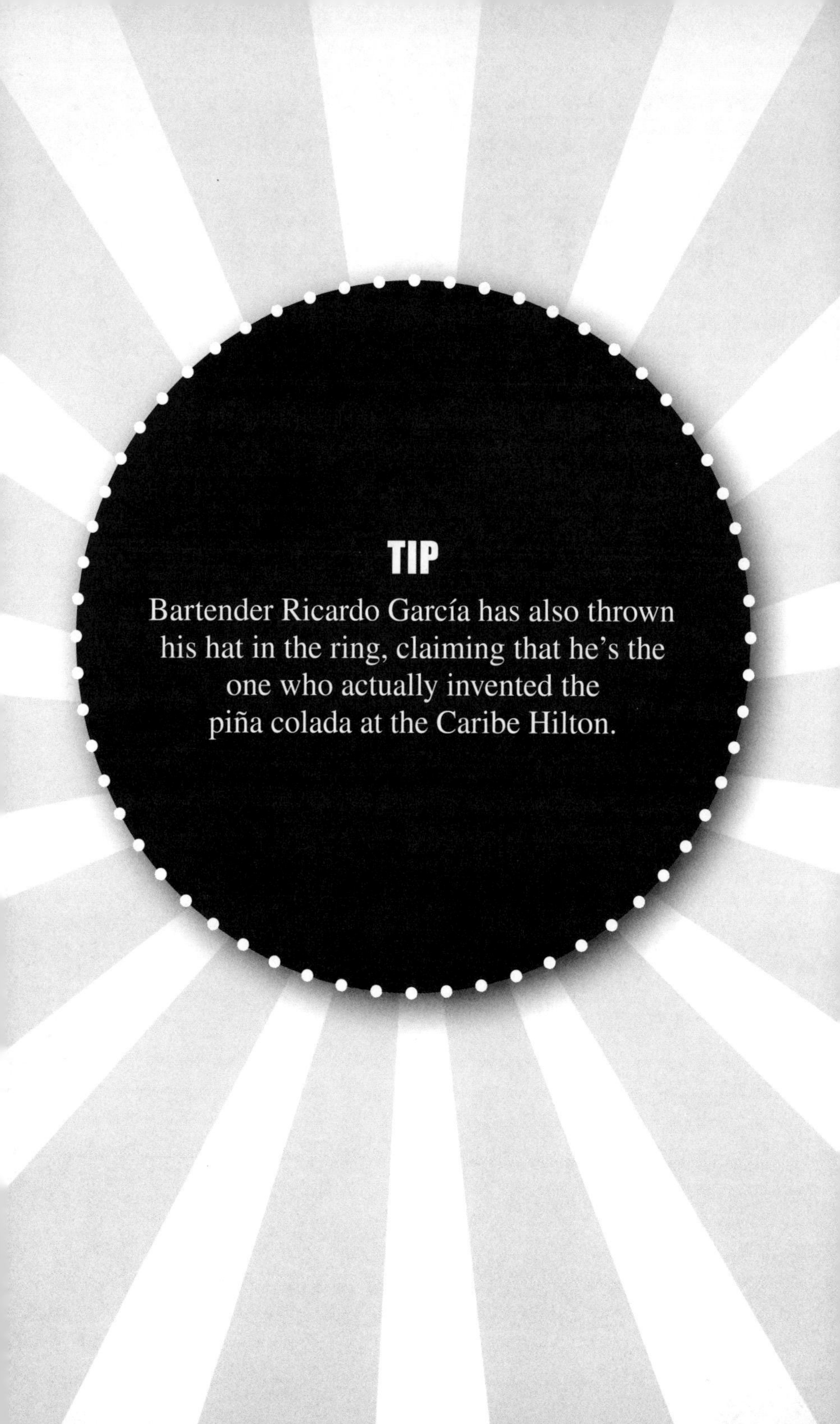

## TIP

Bartender Ricardo García has also thrown his hat in the ring, claiming that he's the one who actually invented the piña colada at the Caribe Hilton.

5

# GORGE ON ROAST PORK
## IN GUAVATE

Your nose lets you know when you're getting close to Guavate, a deliciously famous neighborhood known across the island—and the world—as La Ruta del Lechón (the Roast Pork Route). The area's many *lechoneras* (roast pork restaurants) range from high-capacity cafeteria-style eateries to modest roadside kiosks, all of which line a windy stretch of road in the mountainous municipality of Cayey. A visit to Guavate is a chance to experience Puerto Rican cuisine at its most authentic. You'll see whole pigs roasting slowly on spits over open fires before they're chopped up with machetes and served. The result is a mouthwatering mix of tender meat and salty, crispy skin, which you can gobble up along with sides like fried plantains, rice with pigeon peas, and blood sausage.

Carr. 184, Bo. Guavate
Cayey

While Guavate is relatively quiet during the week, on weekends the entire area becomes a lively street party. Crowds spill out from restaurants and bars packed with families and friends stuffing themselves silly and dancing to live salsa music.

6

# LEARN HOW YOUR COFFEE
## GOES FROM CROP TO CUP

Puerto Rico is famous the world over for its exceptional coffee. The high elevation, nutrient-rich soil, and unique climate of the Cordillera Central mountain range make for ideal growing conditions. Several of the island's coffee farms are open to the public, and Hacienda Tres Ángeles, a 108-acre property in Adjuntas, is a great place to start. Known for its high-quality beans and sustainable practices, the hacienda offers Saturday morning tours where you can learn about the entire coffee-making process, beginning with a walk through the fields and ending with a tasting. Afterwards, you can spend the afternoon hacienda hopping at Café Oro, Lareño Torrefacción, and Hacienda Lealtad, which are all within a half-hour's drive and feature cafés where you can enjoy flavorful brews alongside magnificent mountain views.

**TIP**

If you visit Hacienda Tres Ángeles during harvest season between August and December, you can pick the beans for yourself.

**Hacienda Tres Ángeles**
Carr. 129 km 38.4, Bo. Poerillo, Adjuntas
787-360-0019
haciendatresangeles.com

**Hacienda Lealtad**
Carr. 128 km 51.8, Bo. Buenos Aires, Lares
787-897-8181
cafelealtad.com

**Lareño Torrefacción**
Carr. 128 km 57.7, Bo. La Torre, Lares
787-897-7762
cafelarenopr.com

**Café Oro**
Carr. 129 km 25.4, Bo. Piletas, Lares
939-235-6863
cafeorodepuertorico.com

7

# ASK WHAT'S BEHIND EVERY DOOR

## AT LA FACTORÍA

On the surface, La Factoría is one of Old San Juan's buzziest bars, but dig a little deeper and you'll find that it's so much more. Every door at this hot spot has the potential to reveal an entirely new experience, complete with its own vibe, menu, and style. Enter from the street and order an artisan craft cocktail in the low-key main bar, then hook a left and you'll find yourself in Vino, a refined, candlelit wine bar. Next comes the Shing A Ling Room, where you can dance to live salsa music every Sunday and Monday. But that's not all; keep looking to uncover more unique spaces, like the speakeasy-style El Desvío and El Final, where DJs spin electronic beats into the early morning hours.

148 Calle San Sebastián, Old San Juan
facebook.com/lafactoriapr

### TIP

La Factoría also serves as an informal art gallery. Keep an eye out for everything from graffiti-style paintings to abstract pieces that complement each space.

8

# RAISE A BIERSTEIN
## AT CASA BAVARIA

In 1978, Mike López traveled from Germany to Puerto Rico in search of a father he'd never met, and once he stepped foot on the island, his Borinquen roots told him that he was home. He found his dad, eventually moved his family to Orocovis, and opened Casa Bavaria in 1996. Set in an Alpine-style chalet on the side of a sinuous mountain road, the eatery quickly gained a well-deserved reputation for serving some of the best German food this side of Berlin. Mike's children, Julia and Michael Jr., now run the restaurant, where you can savor the same authentic bratwurst, schnitzel, and strudel that put Casa Bavaria on the map. Add in an impressive selection of imported beer and jaw-dropping panoramic views, and you might never want to leave either.

Carr. 155 km 38.3, Orocovis
787-862-7818
casabavaria.com

**TIP**

Casa Bavaria goes all out for Oktoberfest, when partiers come from across the island on weekends to celebrate with live polka bands, lederhosen-clad servers, and tons of food and beer.

9

# MELT CHEDDAR CHEESE
## INTO YOUR HOT CHOCOLATE AT CHOCOBAR CORTÉS

Satisfy your sweet tooth at Chocobar Cortés, a restaurant and café from the family behind Puerto Rico's Chocolate Cortés, the largest chocolate manufacturer in the Caribbean. Cacao makes an appearance in nearly every dish on the menu, from churros dipped in melted chocolate to salad topped with chocolate vinaigrette. Order a hot chocolate—there are twelve to choose from—and it will come with an unexpected accoutrement: cheddar cheese. The local custom of melting cheese into hot chocolate began in the 1930s as a way for Puerto Ricans to add extra creaminess to their cocoa, and you can continue the tradition today. Drop some cheddar into your cup, give it a stir, and savor a treat that's as smooth as *abuela* (grandma) used to make.

210 Calle San Francisco, Old San Juan
787-722-0499
chocobarcortes.com

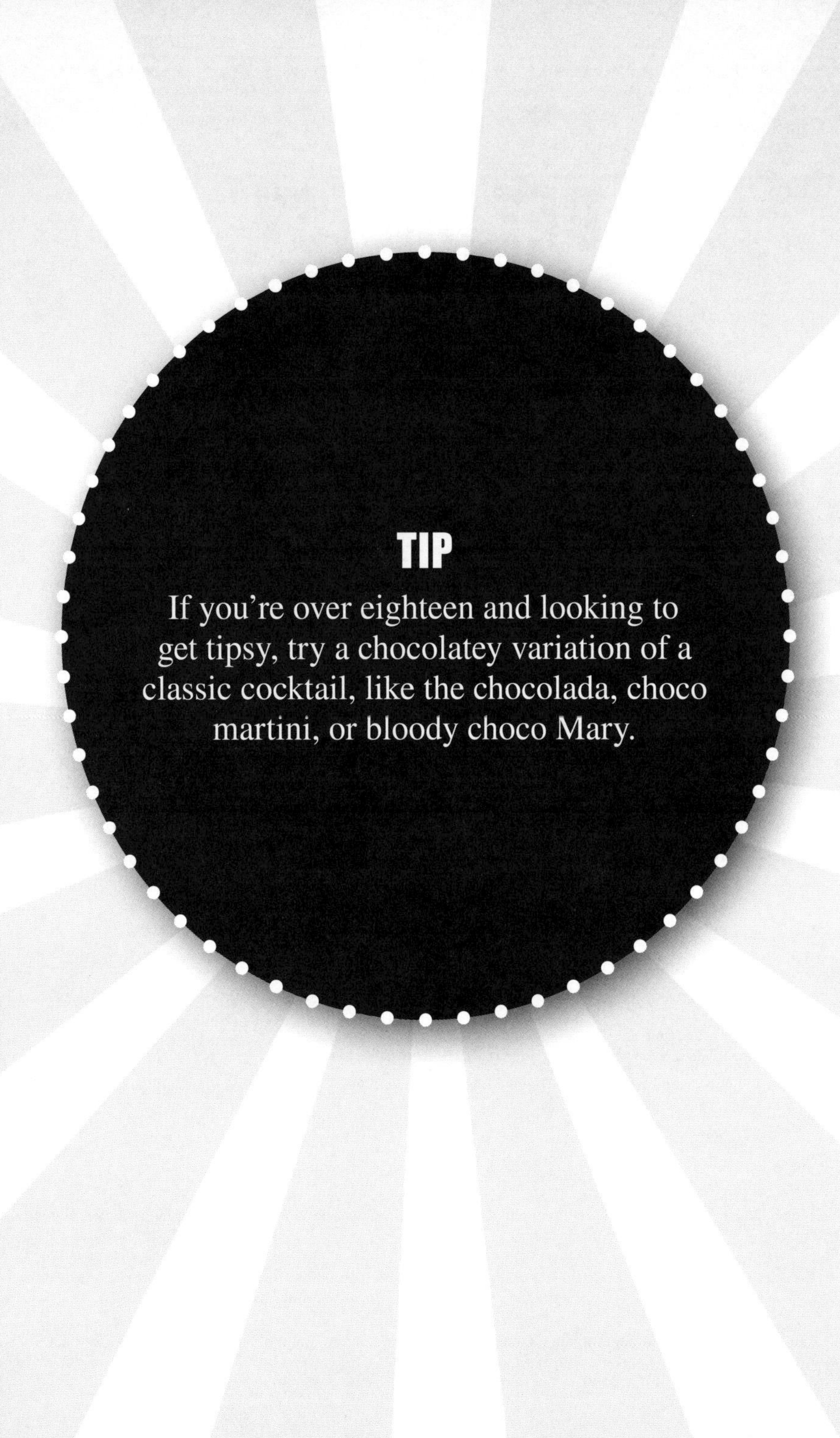

## TIP

If you're over eighteen and looking to get tipsy, try a chocolatey variation of a classic cocktail, like the chocolada, choco martini, or bloody choco Mary.

10

# GET CHEESY
## AT VACA NEGRA

If you're Wanda Otero, when life gives you milk, you learn how to make cheese. A microbiologist by trade, Otero worked in dairy quality control for thirty years. When the 2008 recession hit and her clients couldn't afford to pay, she bartered her services for milk and opened Vaca Negra. Today, the cheese-making operation churns out four hundred pounds of artisan cheese each week in five varieties—cheddar, Beaufort, Gouda, Gruyère, and Manchego—which are sold online, in grocery stores around the island, and at the on-site café at the company's Hatillo headquarters. You can join in the fun during Vaca Negra's two-hour cheese-making classes, where you'll craft your own with your choice of fresh herbs. Once your wheel has aged the two months required by Puerto Rican law, you can pick it up in person or have it shipped to your home.

Carr. 493 km 0.7, Bo. Carrizalez, Hatillo
787-262-5656
vacanegra.com

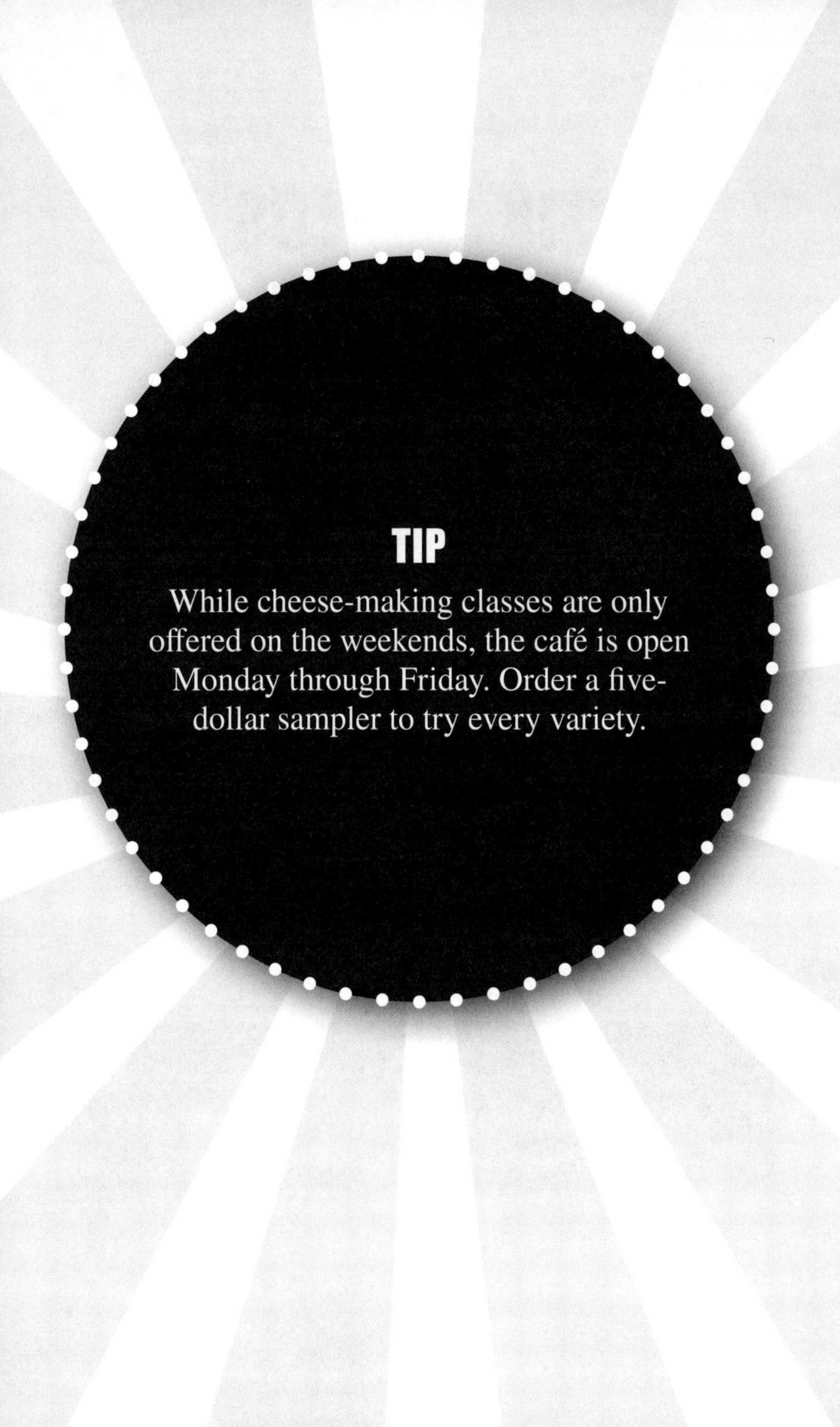

## TIP

While cheese-making classes are only offered on the weekends, the café is open Monday through Friday. Order a five-dollar sampler to try every variety.

11

# MIX MOJITOS
## AT CASA BACARDÍ

Raise a glass to the spirit of Puerto Rico at Casa Bacardí, the headquarters of the world-renowned rum brand since 1958. Located in Cataño, just across the bay from Old San Juan, the distillery opens its doors to the public with guided tours and interactive experiences that offer an insider's peek into Bacardí's origins and its distilling process. A historical tour focuses on the brand's heritage, a tasting tour includes samples of six different rums, and a mixology class puts you behind the bar to learn how to make three classic mixed drinks. All three options start with a complimentary welcome cocktail in the open-air Bat Bar pavilion and end in the gift shop, where you can stock up on Bacardí souvenirs.

Carr. 165 km 6.2, Cataño
787-788-8400
bacardi.com/casa-bacardi

**TIP**

To impress your tour guide and your fellow visitors, pronounce the company name the right way: bah-car-DEE.

12

# EAT RICE AND BEANS FOR DESSERT
## AT HELADERÍA LARES

It all started in 1968, when businessman Don Salvador Barreto opened an *heladería* (ice cream parlor) in his hometown of Lares. While the shop initially served traditional flavors, one day Barreto had an unorthodox idea: corn ice cream. His daring experiment was a rousing success, and since then, Heladería Lares has been the island's go-to destination for deliciously creative treats. While patrons line up around the block to select from a rotating selection of about fifty flavors each day, over the years the store has served more than five hundred unique ice cream concoctions, like rice and beans, avocado, wine, garlic, and codfish. The business closed temporarily in 2014, but it reopened in 2017 and is still operated by Don Salvador's son, Alberto, and grandson, Alberto.

10 Calle Vilella, Lares
787-378-4288
facebook.com/Heladeria-Lares-Oficial-390277911039439/

**TIP**

You're only allowed to sample three flavors before placing your order, so choose wisely.

13

# TRY AS MANY TROPICAL FRUITS

## AS YOU POSSIBLY CAN

Did you know that more than a dozen varieties of mangoes grow in Puerto Rico? Or that, unlike the Hass avocados that you'll find in most American grocery stores, bright green aguacates (Puerto Rican avocados) are shiny and smooth and can easily grow to as big as two pounds? Your body and your taste buds will thank you when you broaden your produce horizons. If you're new to the island or here for a visit, chances are you'll find healthy, delicious fruits you've never heard of, let alone eaten, from acerola to guanabana to tamarind. So go ahead and pick a carambola straight from the tree. Suck on the pit of a quenepa. Cool off with a coco frío on the side of the road. Embracing Puerto Rico's natural flavors will make your time here that much sweeter.

**TIP**

Many restaurants and roadside kiosks serve fresh-squeezed natural juices, so before you order a soda or a beer, ask what else is on the menu.

14

# HANG OUT ON THE SIDE OF THE ROAD
## AT LOS KIOSKOS

In the mood for arepas and mofongo? How about fresh-from-the-oven pizza and calzones? Or locally caught Caribbean lobster and a tall glass of sangría? No matter what you're craving, you're likely to find it at Los Kioskos (the Kiosks) in Luquillo, a roadside strip of more than fifty restaurants, bars, and gift shops that abut Highway 3 to the south and Luquillo Beach to the north. The perfect place to bask in local culture and ogle ocean views, Los Kioskos have been dishing out delicious food and great times for more than seventy years, evolving from palm-frond-laden beach huts to the built-to-last structures that stand today. The atmosphere is usually pretty tame during the week, but on weekends the area turns into a high-energy party scene.

Calle Marginal, Luquillo

**TIP**

Bars stay open until 2 a.m. on Friday and Saturday nights, and on Saturdays and Sundays, the parking lot is packed with hundreds of fun-seekers eating, drinking, and blasting reggaeton from their cars.

# LEARN TO COOK FROM THE BEST
## AT ATELIER AT COCINA ABIERTA

After cutting his teeth in lauded kitchens around the world, in 2010 Chef Martín Louzao opened Cocina Abierta, a hyper-seasonal restaurant with a menu that changes by the week. Six years later he added Atelier, a combination classroom and kitchen where he and his fellow chefs from around the island lead hands-on cooking workshops in which you can embrace your culinary creativity. The space is lined with vintage trinkets and utensils, which makes classes here feel as intimate as if you were hanging out in a friend's kitchen. Topics range from down-home Puerto Rican cuisine to from-scratch pasta to sushi, but no matter which class you choose, you'll leave with a full belly and a handful of tasty recipes to make at home.

58 Calle Caribe, Condado, San Juan
787-946-1333
ateliercocinaabierta.com

**TIP**

Order wine and cocktails from Cocina Abierta during your class, and the restaurant's staff will deliver them right to your seat so that you don't have to miss a minute of instruction.

16

# SAY "SALUD!" WITH COQUITO ON THREE KING'S DAY

Puerto Rico's holiday season doesn't end on New Year's Day. The most important religious event of the year is actually January 6, Three King's Day, which commemorates the three wise men's arrival in Bethlehem. It's a joyous time, and no matter where or with whom you celebrate, no Three King's Day is complete without the creamy, rum-based cocktail known as coquito. Everyone has a version that they swear is the best, but the basic ingredients are always the same: coconut milk, coconut cream, condensed milk, evaporated milk, cinnamon, and rum. Drink your coquito alongside a plateful of pasteles, a signature holiday dish made with meat (usually pork), green plantains, potatoes, and pumpkin, all mixed together, wrapped in a banana leaf, and boiled.

**TIP**

On the eve of Three King's Day, kids fill shoeboxes with grass and put them under the tree to feed the wise men's camels.

17

# DRINK A BEER BORN ON THE BEACH

## AT OCEAN LAB BREWING COMPANY

At Ocean Lab Brewing Company, biochemical engineer turned brewmaster José Carlos González is reinventing Puerto Rico's beer scene one batch at a time. From the citrusy BOB (Blood Orange Blonde) to the bold Ocean Baraka—made with coffee beans farmed in Adjuntas—González and his team produce as much as fifty thousand gallons of premium beer each month, and you can find them in restaurants and bars across the island. To try limited-edition varieties that you won't find anywhere else, visit the company's headquarters in Carolina and ask what's on tap at Ocean Restaurant, which overlooks the aquamarine waters of the Atlantic. While the brewery doesn't offer formal tours (yet), if you ask, you just might get a chance to see the brewing and bottling process for yourself.

Carr. 187 km 2.6, Carolina
787-402-8070
oceanlabbrewery.com

## TIP

Ocean Lab is located in the same complex (and is under the same ownership) as Vivo Beach Club, which includes an oceanfront outdoor concert venue.

18

# PLAY ALL DAY
## ON A *CHINCHORREO*

Weekends and holidays in Puerto Rico bring on one of the island's most popular pastimes. *Chinchorreos* are fun, food-centric road trips of sorts, where groups of family and friends stop at one *chinchorro* (roadside restaurant or bar) after another to enjoy local specialties like alcapurrias and pastelillos, along with drinks, live music, dancing, and games. Seaside dining and entertainment destinations like Piñones in Loíza and La Guancha in Ponce make it easy to park your car and walk between *chinchorros*, or if you prefer to cover more ground, you can drive along loosely mapped routes in mountain towns like Aibonito and Cayey or stop at beachy shacks and kiosks in coastal areas like Barceloneta and Aguadilla.

Piñones
Bo. Carolina, Loíza

La Guancha
Calle C, Ponce

Chinchorreo Bus
787-998-5466
facebook.com/Chinchorreobus

19

# BUY A *PIRAGUA*
## FROM A PUSHCART

If you're hanging out in the park or on the beach on a hot day and you hear a ringing bell getting louder and louder, you're in for a (frozen) treat; the *piraguas* cart is headed your way! It's hard not to smile when you're eating this shaved-ice dessert, which is a bit like a sno-cone with a Puerto Rican spin. The vendors, or *piragüeros*, who push the carts and hand-shave the ice are often well-known fixtures in the towns where they work. You'll see kids and adults buying a cup to cool off from the Caribbean sun. Flavor your *piragua* with fruity syrups like coconut, passionfruit, pineapple, and tamarind, then do your best to finish it all before it melts.

**TIP**

Piragua gets its name from its distinctive conic shape. *Pir* comes from *pirámide*, which means "pyramid", and *agua* means "water.

# SIP THE PIRATE AT SUNSET
## AT VILLA COFRESÍ

As the saying goes, if you haven't tried the Pirate, you haven't been to Rincón. Served in a coconut—as all iconic Caribbean cocktails should be—the famous concoction was conceived in 1965 at Villa Cofresí. Decades later, it remains the most popular item on the hotel's menu. Grab a seat at the beachfront bar and watch in anticipation as your bartender hacks open a coconut with a machete and fills it with a mixture of four types of rum, fresh coconut water, and evaporated milk. Topped with a sprinkle of cinnamon, the dangerously delicious cocktail makes its way to you to sip and savor. You can order the Pirate at any hour, but somehow it tastes just a little bit sweeter against the backdrop of those famous Rincón sunsets.

Carr. 115 km 12, Rincón
787-823-2450
villacofresi.com

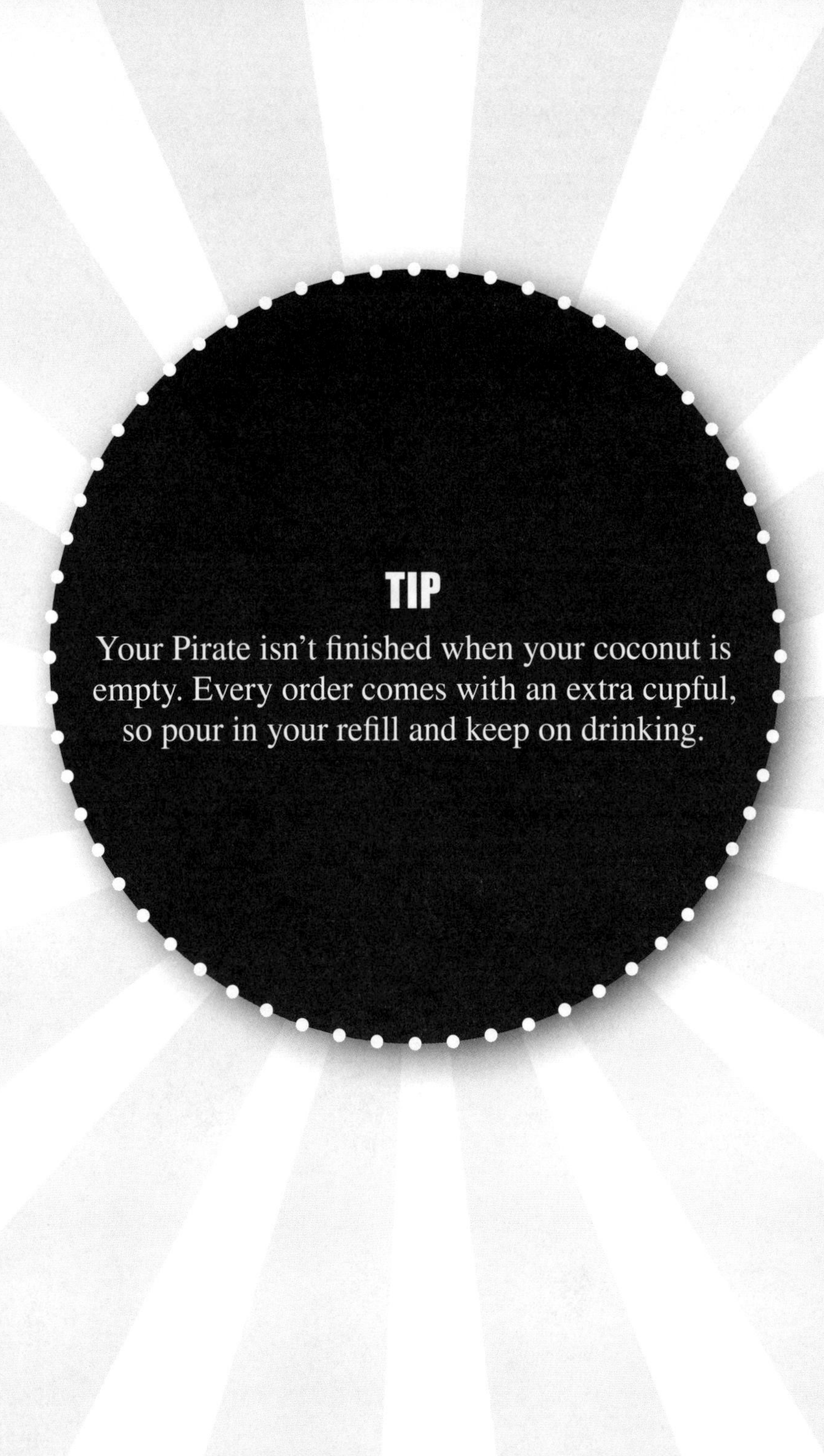

## TIP

Your Pirate isn't finished when your coconut is empty. Every order comes with an extra cupful, so pour in your refill and keep on drinking.

La Factoría
(Photo Credit: Karina Margary Photography)

# MUSIC AND ENTERTAINMENT

21

# JOIN THE PARTY
## AT LA PLACITA DE SANTURCE

*Placita* translates to "little plaza," but the action at this Santurce hot spot is anything but small. During the day, an open-air farmer's market bustles with vendors selling produce of all kinds and colors, but Thursday, Friday, and Saturday nights bring one of the liveliest nightlife scenes on the island. The area's chic, chef-driven restaurants, combined with a mix of trendy and divey bars, draw a diverse crowd with a common goal: fun. Join the fray and hop from bar to bar to enjoy cold beer, potent cocktails, live music, DJs, and more. La Placita also hosts free concerts throughout the year, and people come in droves to dance to salsa, bomba, and other Latin beats.

179 Calle Dos Hermanos, Santurce, San Juan

**TIP**

Don't leave without snapping an Instagram-worthy photo with the giant metal avocado sculptures.

22

# PLAY
## THE (WOODEN) PONIES

Get your dollar bills ready for pica, a gambling game that's a bit like a carnival-ized combination of roulette and horse racing. Its name is derived from the Spanish word *hípica* (equestrian), and it's been one of Puerto Rico's most fun and authentic pastimes for more than one hundred years. As an operator turns a crank that moves twenty-four (sometimes thirty) wooden horses around a circular track, players crowd around the board and throw down their bets on which horse will come to a stop closest to—but without crossing—the finish line. While gambling is usually permitted only at licensed venues, pica is legal everywhere.

### TIP

You can almost always find pica at Patronales festivals, where you can celebrate each municipality's patron saint with food trucks, rides, games, and music.

23

# DANCE UNTIL THE SUN COMES UP

## AT BRAVA NIGHTCLUB

Anyone who's anyone has partied at Brava Nightclub in Isla Verde's posh El San Juan hotel. The venue first opened in the 1950s as Hunka Munka, and while it has been called by many names since (Babylon, Amadeus), it has never lost its cachet as the place for late-night dancing, drinking, and good times. Jennifer Lopez hosted her first album release party here, Beyoncé and Jay-Z have been known to stop by, and Bad Bunny even performed live in the five-thousand-square-foot space. Brava opens at 10 p.m. on Thursday, Friday, and Saturday and stays packed for hours, so don't be surprised if the sun's already up by the time you walk out the door.

6063 Avenida Isla Verde, Carolina
787-791-2781
elsanjuanhotel.com/entertainment/brava

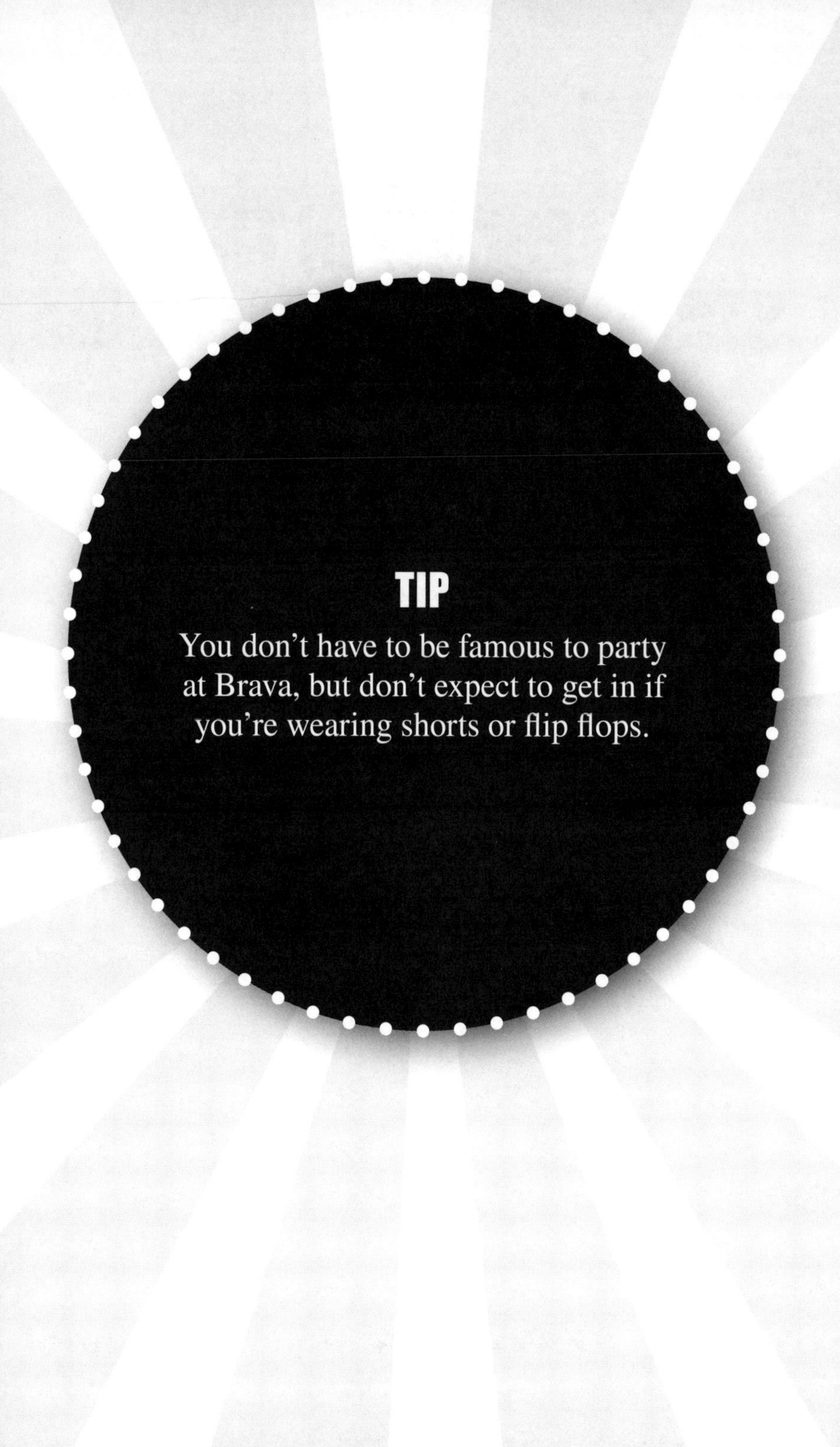

## TIP

You don't have to be famous to party at Brava, but don't expect to get in if you're wearing shorts or flip flops.

# CELEBRATE IN THE STREETS OF OLD SAN JUAN DURING SANSE

If you ask anyone in Puerto Rico about the biggest party of the year, you'll hear one answer: the San Sebastián Festival. Every year in mid-January, SanSe transforms Old San Juan into a massive, multiday event where hundreds of thousands of people celebrate with food, drinks, music, and culture. During the day, you'll see families enjoying kid-friendly entertainment, shopping for handmade crafts and art from local artisans, and cheering as parades of *cabezudos* (big heads) march joyfully through the cobblestone streets. At night, the vibe changes to an alcohol-fueled extravaganza, with loads of food kiosks, bars packed to capacity, and some of the hottest bands and singers in Puerto Rico performing on stages set up in the city's most famous plazas.

Old San Juan
sanjuanciudadpatria.com/eventos

Road closures and heavy traffic make it difficult to get into and out of Old San Juan during SanSe. To save yourself the stress, take the ferry over from Cataño or park your car at Sagrado Corazón train station and hop a bus into the city.

25

# SEE A MOVIE THE OLD-FASHIONED WAY
## AT AUTO CINE SANTANA

In the age of on-demand streaming, Auto Cine Santana puts the magic back into the movie-going experience. At this old-timey drive-in theater, two massive outdoor screens show new releases ranging from kid-friendly cartoons to big-budget blockbusters. When you pull up to the entrance, the attendant working the gate will direct you to the right screen, where you'll join rows of other parked cars. Tune your car radio to the right frequency to hear your movie's audio soundtrack. From there, all that's left to do is sit back, relax, and enjoy the show.

Carr. 662 km 0.5, Bo. Santana, Arecibo
facebook.com/AutoCineSantanaArecibo

**TIP**

Since no movie is complete without popcorn, buy a bag at the snack bar, which also sells sodas, juices, and light bites.

# LISTEN TO THE PLAYER PIANO
## AT THE GALLERY INN

The moment you step foot inside the Gallery Inn, you know you're somewhere special, and you're not sure where to look first. There's a live macaw perched regally on a gargoyle statue, bronze busts in the likenesses of Barack and Michelle Obama, and paintings covering nearly every inch of the exposed-brick walls that have stood here since the seventeenth century—and that's all before you make it past the front desk. This enchanting hotel is the creation of Jan D'Esopo, who, along with her late husband Manuco, is responsible for all the art you see throughout the mazelike, twenty-seven-room inn. Even if you're not staying over, make time for a drink at the Cannon Club, where two gorgeous Steinway player pianos fill the room with song as the bartender fills your glass.

204 Calle Norzagaray, Old San Juan
787-722-1808
thegalleryinn.com

**TIP**

The hotel's rooftop is the highest point in Old San Juan, offering panoramic views of both the city and the ocean.

27

# SEE EL GRAN COMBO PERFORM LIVE

You can't have a conversation about Puerto Rican music without talking about El Gran Combo, arguably the most successful salsa band ever assembled. Pianist Rafael Ithier founded the group in 1962, and while many members have cycled in and out over the years, the Grammy Award-winning ensemble continues to play to sold-out crowds and serve as unofficial ambassadors from Puerto Rico to the world. When you see them live, you won't be able to resist tapping your feet and moving your hips as more than a dozen talented musicians take to the stage and put on a high-energy show. For a schedule of upcoming performances and to buy tickets, search for the band on Ticketmaster.

**TIP**

In its nearly sixty-year history, El Gran Combo has recorded more than seventy albums. You can stream the group's music online to hear a piece of Puerto Rican history.

28

# DANCE, DRINK, AND SHOOT OYSTERS
## IN BOQUERÓN

If you're looking for a party in Cabo Rojo, you'll find it at El Poblado in Boquerón. On weekend nights, this pedestrian-friendly promenade is the place to see and be seen, with both locals and tourists letting loose and having a fantastic time. A handful of restaurants are scattered among lively bars blasting high-decibel tunes that reverberate into the street, and strangers quickly become friends as they dance together to live salsa music and play bar games. The beer and booze flow freely into the wee hours of the night while vendors in kiosks sell fresh-from-the-sea raw clams and oysters. Add a squeeze of lemon and a dash of *pique* (hot sauce), then shoot your shellfish to get the full Boquerón experience.

El Poblado, Bo. Boquerón, Cabo Rojo

### TIP

Many bars in Boquerón serve modified versions of *chichaítos* (traditional shots made with Puerto Rican rum and anisette) that incorporate passionfruit, coconut, and other tropical flavors.

29

# THROW DOWN SOME BONES

## IN A GAME OF DOMINOES

Wherever you are in Puerto Rico, you're never far from the next game of dominoes. All over the islands, you'll see everyone from energetic teenagers to weathered old-timers throwing down bones at the beach, at the bar, in the park, or anywhere that they can set up a table and four chairs. If you're new to the game, the best way to learn is to watch, but it helps to know the basics. Everyone starts with seven dominoes and takes turns matching up numbers on the board until one person (the winner) is out of tiles. It might sound simple, but while knowing how to play is one thing, mastering the game is quite another.

**TIP**

For a great glimpse of authentic domino culture, head to Plaza Colón in Old San Juan, where crowds gather to watch the intense games.

30

# SEE A WORLD-CLASS PERFORMANCE
## AT CENTRO DE BELLAS ARTES

Centro de Bellas Artes made headlines in January 2019 as the venue for Lin-Manuel Miranda's sold-out run of *Hamilton*, but this renowned performing arts center is far from a one-hit wonder. Since 1981, the four-theater complex in Santurce has attracted talented artists from all over the island—and all over the world—who come to share their music, dance, and theatrical works with the people of Puerto Rico. This is the place to be if you want to be dazzled by everything from the Puerto Rico Symphony Orchestra's annual staging of *George Balanchine's The Nutcracker* to the Casals Festival in March, when more than thirty groups from around the globe partake in one of the island's most important and joyful artistic events.

22 Avenida Ponce de León, Santurce, San Juan
787-724-4747
cba.pr.gov

### TIP

You can purchase tickets to performances at Centro de Bellas Artes at the box office, by phone (787-620-4444), or online (cba.pr.gov/boleteria).

31

# CHEER FOR THE NEXT WAVE OF BASEBALL SUPERSTARS

When Major League Baseball's season ends, Puerto Rico's Winter League begins. If you're a fan of the game, you can root for the home team between November and January. The league, officially named the Liga de Béisbol Profesional Roberto Clemente, is an incubator for the MLB, and it's where superstars like Javier Báez, Carlos Correa, and Enrique Hernández stepped up to the plate at the start of their careers. The league's three teams hail from Santurce (los Cangrejeros), Caguas (los Crillos), and Mayagüez (los Indios). While most MLB stadiums have a capacity of more than forty thousand, the stadiums in the Winter League only seat between five thousand and twelve thousand people, so you're never far from the action.

mlb.com/mlb/events/winterleagues

**TIP**

You can purchase tickets at each stadium or buy them online at ticketpluspr.com.

32

# LET THE COQUÍ FROGS LULL YOU TO SLEEP

It only takes one night in Puerto Rico to get to know the coquí, a nocturnal tree frog with a distinctive chirp that provides the island's unofficial lullaby. If you've never heard a coquí's call before, you might think you're listening to birds, but make no mistake, the high-volume soundtrack actually belongs to a male amphibian. Seventeen species of coquí are native to Puerto Rico, but only two of them make the sound that gives the frogs their name: the "ko" warns other males to stay out of his territory, and the "kee" serves to attract females. You might find the cacophony startling at first, but it won't be long before their evening song becomes music to your ears.

**TIP**

While coquíes grow to only about an inch in size, they emit a sound that can reach as high as one hundred decibels, making them the world's loudest amphibian.

Domes Beach in Rincón
(Photo Credit: Victor M. Velázquez / Evo Photography)

# SPORTS AND RECREATION

33

# EXPLORE THE NATURAL TREASURES OF EL YUNQUE NATIONAL FOREST

You can spot the cloud-shrouded peaks of the Luquillo Mountains from miles away, guiding you to El Yunque, a twenty-eight-thousand-acre protected expanse where natural wonders abound. This subtropical rainforest, the only one of its kind in the US National Forest System, receives an annual average of fifteen feet of rainfall, fostering a habitat where a wide variety of flora and fauna thrive. You'll see rainbow-colored orchids and thousand-year-old trees, listen to the calls of coqui frogs and tropical birds, enjoy active adventures like hiking the El Toro Wilderness Trail, and take in impressive sights like the cascading waters of La Coca Falls. And while certain parts of the forest are still off limits as they recover from the devastating 2017 hurricane season, new areas are reopening to the public every month.

El Yunque National Forest
Carr. 191 km 4.4, Rio Grande
fs.usda.gov/elyunque
facebook.com/elyunquenf

Portalito HUB Visitor Center
54 Calle Principal, Bo. Palmer,
Rio Grande
787-888-1880

Check the El Yunque Facebook page or stop by the Portalito HUB Visitor Center for the latest updates on what's open. You can also download the El Yunque National Forest app for free on your mobile device.

# GAZE THROUGH A WINDOW TO THE WORLD

## AT CUEVA VENTANA

No matter how many times you visit Cueva Ventana, the experience never fails to take your breath away. The back side of this cave in Arecibo features a naturally framed porthole that looks down onto the valley below, giving the awe-inspiring formation its name, which translates to "window cave." The only way to access the cave is on a group tour. Over the course of your forty-five-minute journey, you'll get a history lesson as your guide points out drawings and petroglyphs etched into the walls by the Taíno Indians centuries ago, and you'll learn about the plants and animals that live here. Tours are limited to just twenty-five people, so on weekends or during busy times of the year, arrive early to limit your wait time.

PR-10 km 75, Bo. Hato Viejo, Arecibo
787-322-3554
cuevaventanapr.com

### TIP

To get a different perspective, follow PR-123 to the valley below, where you can view the cave from the outside. Below it you'll also spot Cueva León, where drawings of lions offer evidence that African slaves hid there.

35

# HANG TEN
## IN RINCÓN, AGUADILLA, AND ISABELA

You'll see a surfboard strapped to the roof or sticking out the window of nearly every car on the road in Rincón, Aguadilla, and Isabela, three laid-back beach towns on Puerto Rico's northwest corner. Surfers make the pilgrimage here from all over the world to ride the Atlantic Ocean's epic waves. Conditions vary from day to day at more than a dozen beaches along the coast, like Domes and Pools in Rincón, Bridges and Wilderness in Aguadilla, and Shacks and Middles in Isabela. You can catch swells here all year long, but September through November and April through May are considered the height of surfing season.

**TIP**

If you're new to the sport, the relatively predictable waves at Jobos Beach in Isabela make it a great place for beginners to learn. Sign up for a lesson at Volcom Surf School, located right on the beach.

# UNPLUG
## ON ISLA DE MONA

Adventure awaits you on Isla de Mona (Mona Island), an untamed wilderness forty-one miles west of Mayagüez. You'll find no modern facilities here—no bathrooms, cell signal, or even electricity; in fact, pre-Columbian-era Taíno petroglyphs are among the only evidence you'll see of human interference. The largely uninhabited island showcases the natural world in its purest form, with hidden beaches, elaborate cave systems, and a plethora of wildlife, including seventeen species endemic only to Mona. The Department of Natural and Environmental Resources regulates the number of people allowed here at any one time, but you can reserve a spot on a three- or four-night camping trip with Acampa, the only officially sanctioned tour operator. Their expert guides take groups all over Mona and provide everything you need, from food (and a chef!) to tents.

Acampa Nature Adventures
787-706-0695
acampapr.com

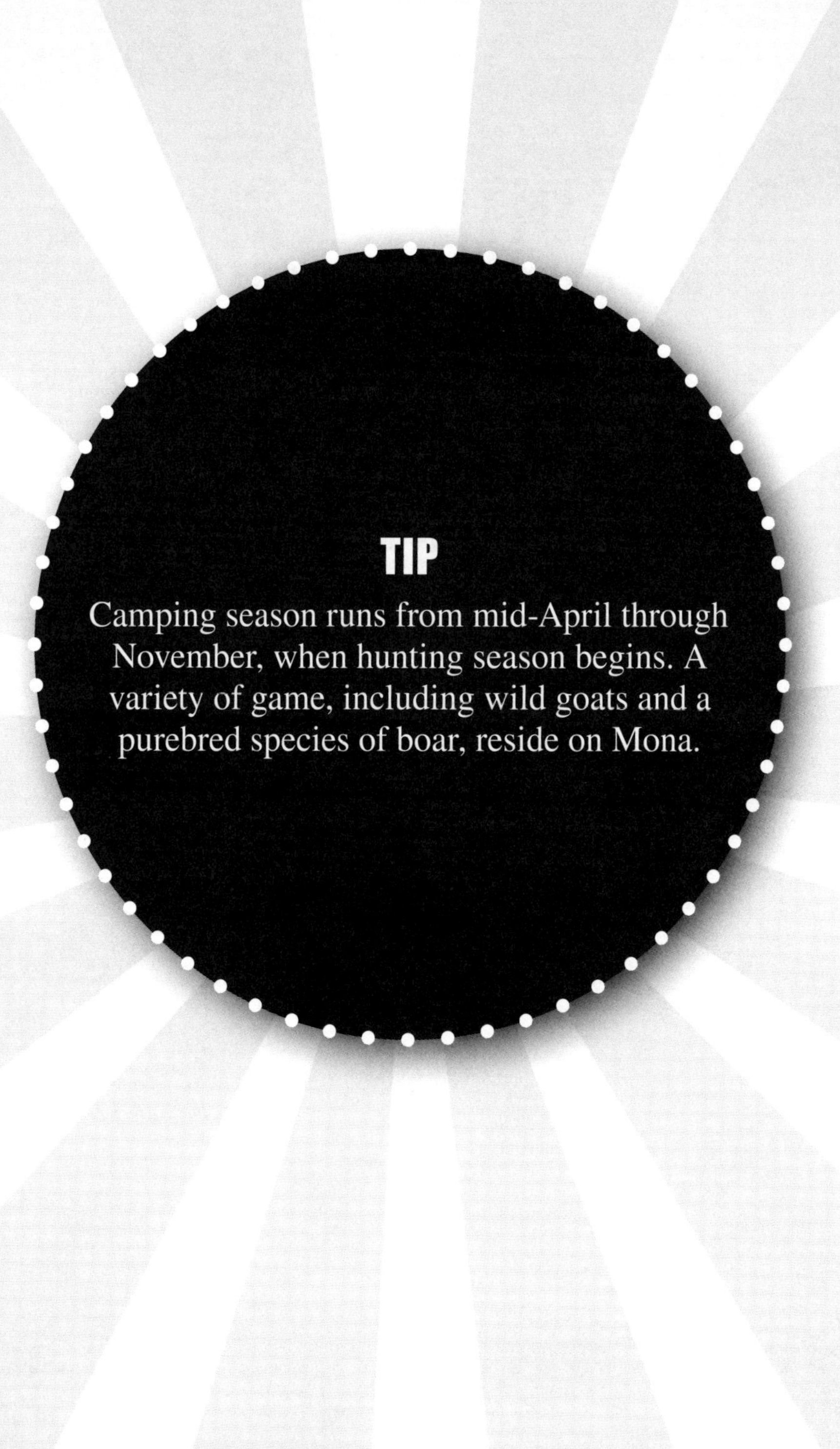

## TIP

Camping season runs from mid-April through November, when hunting season begins. A variety of game, including wild goats and a purebred species of boar, reside on Mona.

# STARE INTO THE DEPTHS
## OF CAÑÓN DE SAN CRISTÓBAL

When you stand at the edge of Cañón de San Cristóbal and behold its grandeur, it's hard to believe that until the 1970s, this natural attraction was used as a dumping ground for garbage from the surrounding towns. Now protected by the Conservation Trust of Puerto Rico and overseen by Para la Naturaleza, a nonprofit conservation organization, the 5.6-mile canyon between Barranquitas and Aibonito has been restored to its rightful state of uncompromised beauty. Slowly carved from solid rock over millions of years, the chasm plunges to depths of 750 feet in some places and features more than seven hundred species of plants and wildlife, along with rivers, ponds, and Salto La Vaca, the tallest waterfall in Puerto Rico.

PR-725, Aibonito/Barranquitas
787-722-5882
paralanaturaleza.org/en/canon-san-cristobal

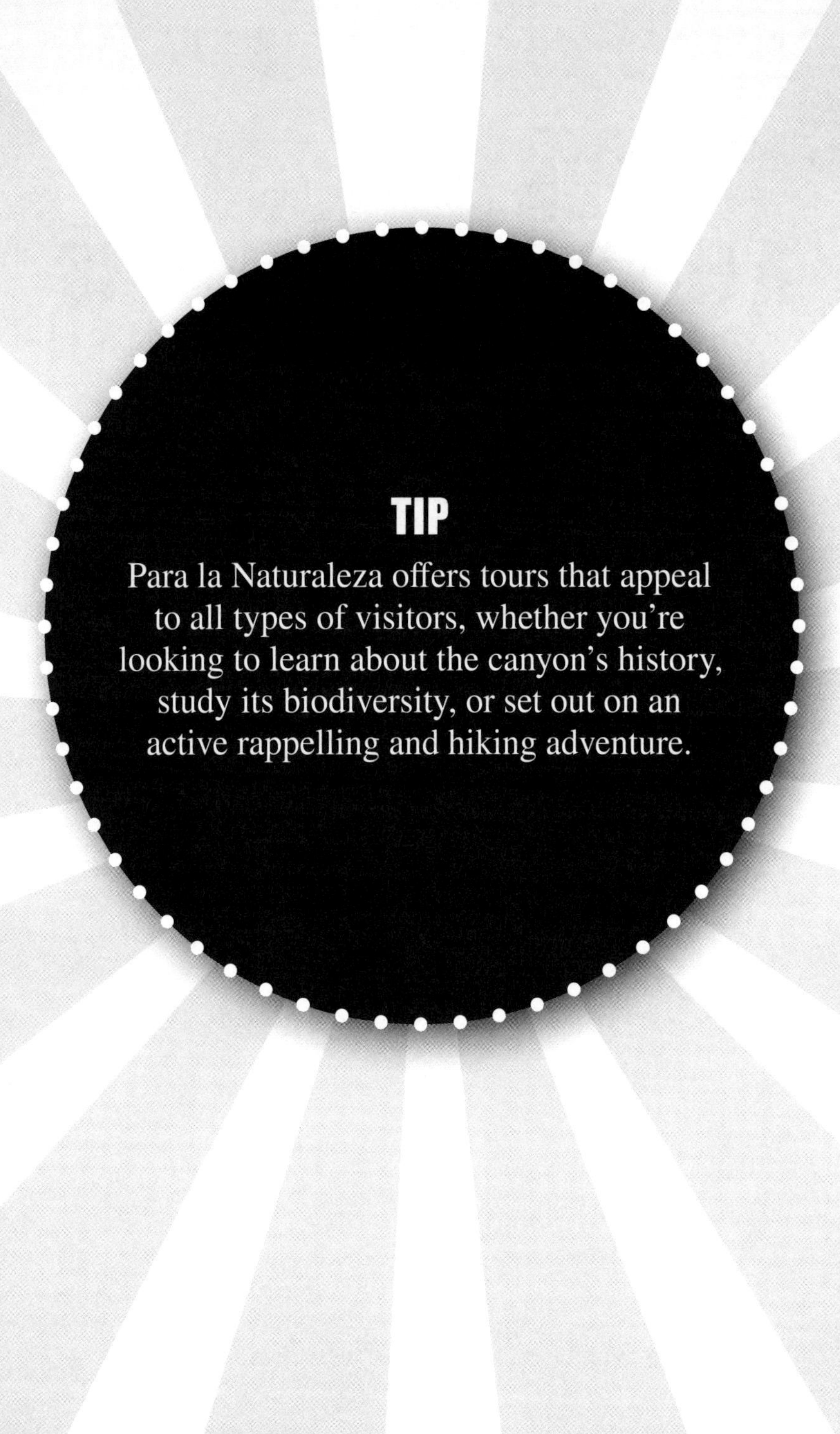
TIP
Para la Naturaleza offers tours that appeal to all types of visitors, whether you're looking to learn about the canyon's history, study its biodiversity, or set out on an active rappelling and hiking adventure.

# RUN THROUGH A FIELD OF SUNFLOWERS

## AT FINCA EL GIRASOL

Finca El Girasol translates to Sunflower Farm, and that's exactly what you'll find at this floral oasis in Guánica. The fifteen-acre working farm cultivates tens of thousands of sunflowers, punctuating the surrounding landscape with a cheerful pop of orange and yellow that eagle-eyed passersby can spot from Highway 116. The property is open to visitors seven days a week, and most guests spend about forty-five minutes strolling through the fields, snapping photos, and admiring the colorful array. The area's stable climate enables the plants to thrive year-round, so there's always something to see. Picking the sunflowers yourself is off limits, but you can buy freshly cut blooms at the on-site farm stand, which also sells fruits and vegetables from neighboring growers.

PR-116, Guánica
939-402-7967
facebook.com/Finca-El-Girasol-587771284669485/

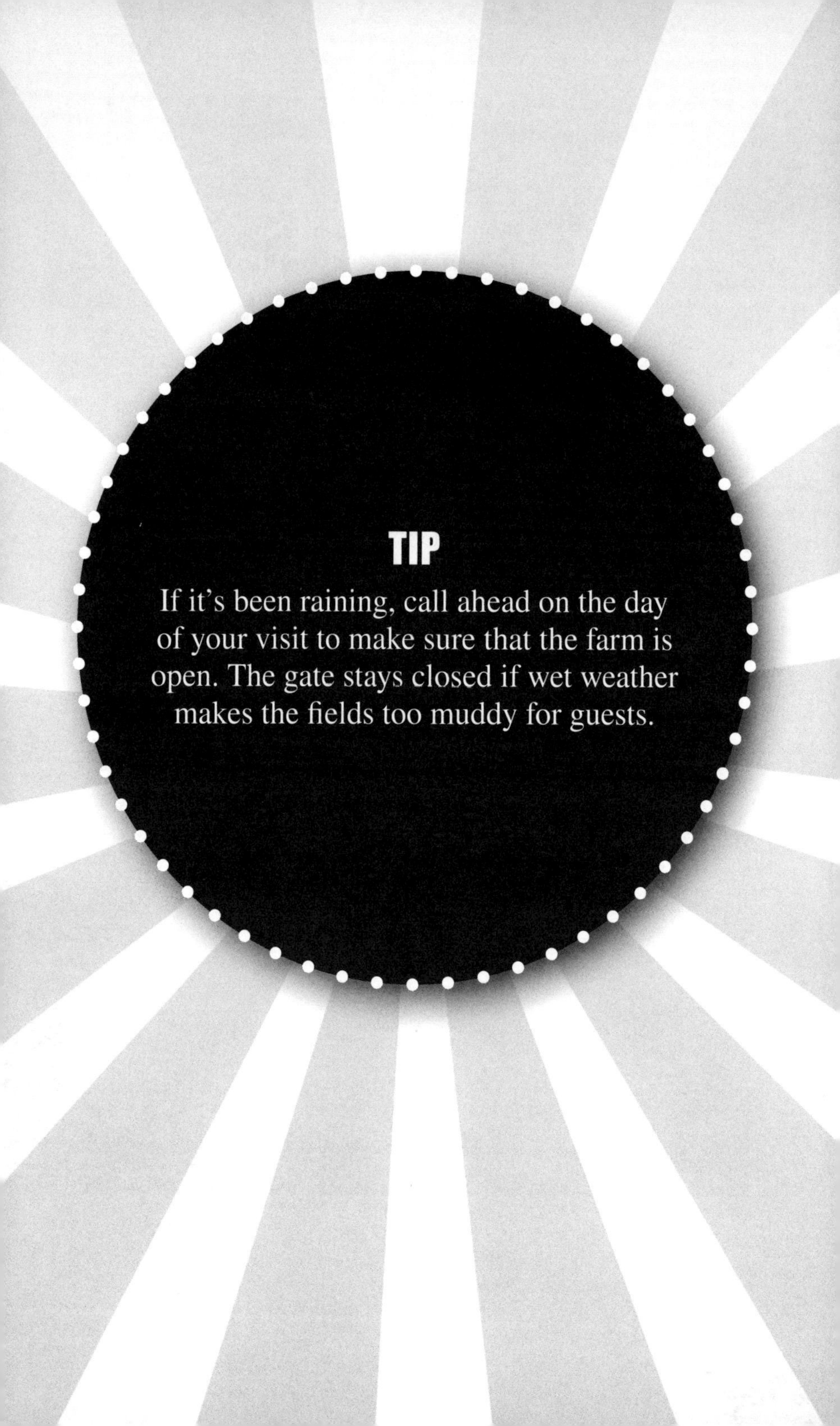

## TIP

If it's been raining, call ahead on the day of your visit to make sure that the farm is open. The gate stays closed if wet weather makes the fields too muddy for guests.

39

# SWIM WITH SEA TURTLES
## AT PLAYA TORTUGA

If you haven't been snorkeling or scuba diving in Puerto Rico, then you are missing out on half of what makes this place so special. With healthy coral reefs and relatively unpolluted waters, the islands provide an inviting habitat for a slew of marine life, including three types of sea turtles. You can swim among them at Playa Tortuga (Turtle Beach) on the offshore paradise of Culebrita, a popular breeding ground for green sea turtles. Watching them glide underwater is at once beautiful, thrilling, and unforgettable. To get there, you can hop in a water taxi from Culebra, or better yet, make a day of it with a catamaran trip with Paz Vela Charters, which includes stops at several beaches on the island.

Paz Vela Charters
787-215-3809
culebracatamaran.com

### TIP

The calm, shallow tidal pools on the north end of Playa Tortuga are known as the Jacuzzis, and and they're the perfect spot to soak up the sun as you relax in the warm water.

40

# MASTER THE MONSTER

## AT TOROVERDE ADVENTURE PARK

If you're ready to feel the adrenaline rush that comes from soaring through the air Superman-style at ninety-five miles per hour, head to Toroverde Adventure Park and strap in for a ride on the Monster. This zip line high in the mountains of Orocovis spans nearly two miles, making it the longest of its kind in the western hemisphere. (The longest in the world is at Toroverde in the United Arab Emirates.) Even reluctant daredevils get a thrill from the flight; within moments, trepidation gives way to exhilaration as you gaze at the lush mountains, deep ravines, and wide-open skies around you. The largest adventure park in the Caribbean, Toroverde also features the Beast, a zip line that spans just under a mile, as well as eight traditional zip lines and four suspension bridges.

Carr. 155 km 33, Bo. Gato, Orocovis
787-867-7100
toroverdepr.com

**TIP**

Be sure to wear closed-toed athletic shoes. If you show up in flip flops or sandals, you won't be allowed to participate.

41

# SEE THE NORTH AND SOUTH COASTS
## FROM CERRO DE PUNTA

Set within the protected wilderness of Toro Negro State Forest, Cerro de Punta towers over Puerto Rico from 4,390 feet above sea level. And while it's no surprise that the highest peak in Puerto Rico has spectacular views, observing them in person will leave you awestruck. On a clear day, you can see all the way to Arecibo on the island's north shore and Ponce on the southern coast, and you might even be able to spot San Juan seventy-five miles away. You can reach the base of the mountain from either Ponce or Jayuya, and while you'll drive most of the way, you'll have to walk the last portion. Be aware; the road is steep, narrow, and potholed, so only attempt to make it to the top in an all-wheel-drive vehicle.

Bosque Estatal de Toro Negro<br>(Toro Negro State Forest)<br>Carr. 143 km 17.2, Ponce/Jayuya

TIP

Unlike the tropical climate of Puerto Rico at sea level, temperatures here can drop into the forties (Fahrenheit) in the winter. Dress accordingly.

42

# KAYAK THROUGH WATER THAT GLOWS IN THE DARK

## IN VIEQUES

When the sun goes down, Puerto Mosquito on the island of Vieques brings the magic. Okay, it's technically science, but it certainly feels like magic. This bay contains an unusually high concentration of microorganisms called dinoflagellates, which illuminate in response to movement in the water. In fact, Puerto Mosquito holds the Guinness World Record as the brightest bioluminescent bay in the world, and the effect is nothing short of wondrous. These tiny creatures emit a bright blue glow that mesmerizes onlookers, only to dissipate just a second later. Several companies run nightly kayaking tours, and most include a biology crash course that will help you understand what you're seeing and why Puerto Mosquito provides the ideal environment for this enchanting phenomenon.

Taíno Aqua Adventures
787-349-6964
tainoaquaadventures.com

JAK Water Sports
787-644-7112
jakwatersports.com

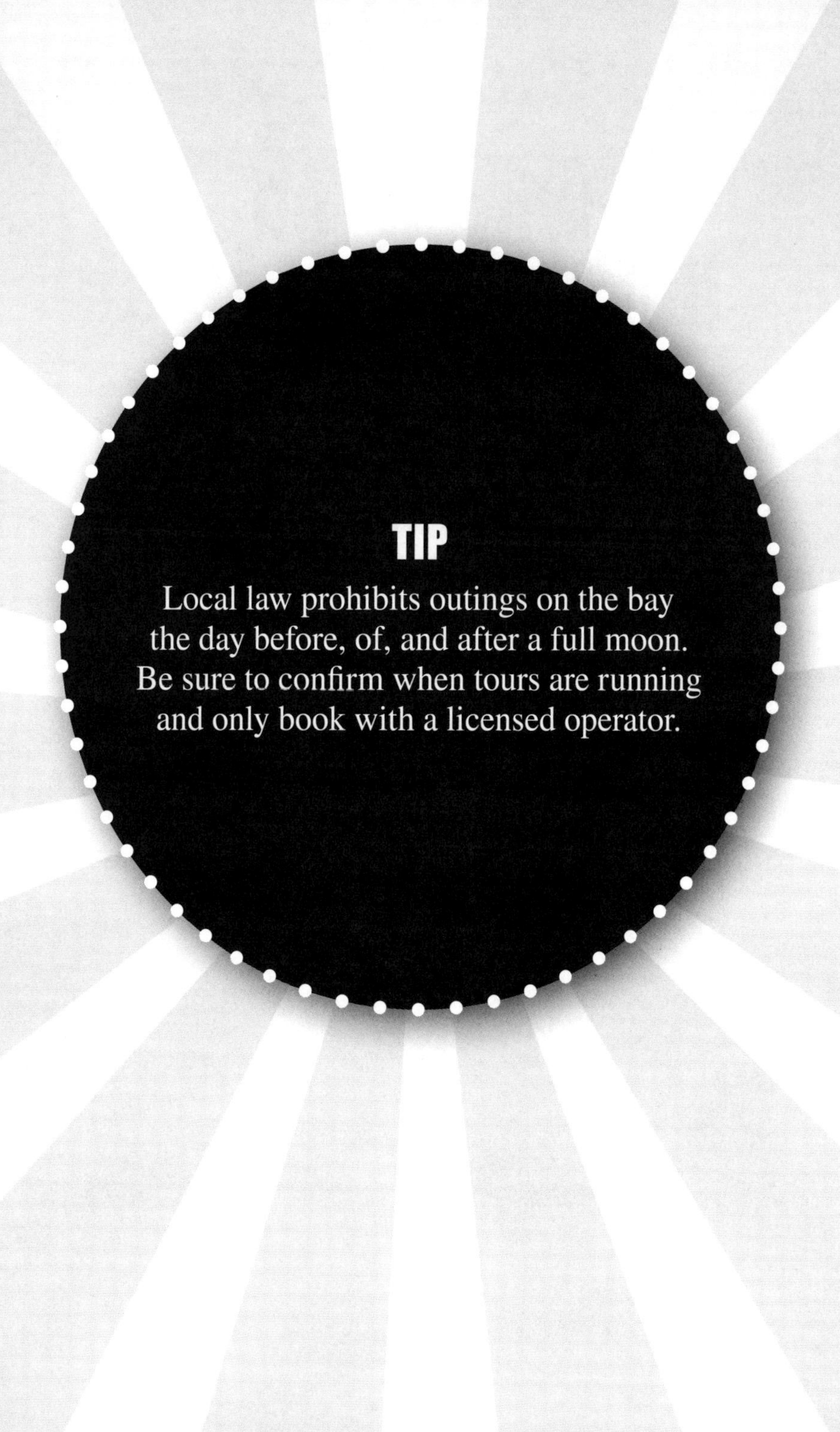

## TIP

Local law prohibits outings on the bay the day before, of, and after a full moon. Be sure to confirm when tours are running and only book with a licensed operator.

43

# WATCH FOR HUMPBACK WHALES
## IN THE PORTA DEL SOL

Humans aren't the only mammals that migrate to the Caribbean for the winter. Every year between January and March, thousands of humpback whales pass through the warm waters off Puerto Rico on their way to spend the summer in the north Atlantic Ocean. These magnificent beasts, which can grow to as long as fifty feet and weigh an astounding fifty tons, come here to mate and calve, and if you're lucky, you might catch a glimpse of them when they rise to the surface for air. This endangered species has been spotted from coastal areas all over Puerto Rico, but your best chance to see them—and hear their mating songs—is just after sunrise or before sunset in the Porta del Sol, which stretches from Cabo Rojo to Isabela.

**TIP**

Humpback whales are far more elusive in the Caribbean than they are in New England and other points north. Go to facebook.com/PRWhales for updates on the most recent sightings.

# FLOAT DOWNSTREAM
## ON THE RÍO TANAMÁ

Amidst the rolling hills of the karst region in western Puerto Rico, the Río Tanamá (Tanama River) winds its way through the municipalities of Arecibo, Utuado, and Adjuntas. While the river is ripe for all kinds of adventure, Explora, a local tour operator, created a trademarked sport that you can only experience right here in Puerto Rico: Body Rafting. These guided excursions begin with a hike through dense woods, and from there you'll rappel down to the river. Once in the water, you'll float on your back using just your body and your life jacket to stay buoyant. As the current carries you downstream, you'll gaze up at nature at its finest, with towering canyons, stalactite-laden caves, and lush greenery, before you hike back up to dry land for a late lunch.

787-900-7755
explorapr.com

### TIP

Explora provides round-trip transportation from San Juan, which takes about an hour and a half each way. You can also join the group at the designated meeting point in Arecibo.

45

# CHASE THE SUN
## FROM THE EAST TO THE WEST

You can easily drive the 106 miles from one end of Puerto Rico to the other in just a few hours, but where's the fun in that? Instead, make a day of it, literally. Start on the east coast in areas like Ceiba, Humacao, or Yabucoa, where you can watch the sun come up over the horizon between 5:50 and 7 a.m., depending on the time of year. From there, head west and plan to arrive at your final destination between 6 and 7 p.m. for sunset. The unobstructed views from spots like the Punta Higuero Lighthouse in Rincón, Buyé Beach in Cabo Rojo, and Las Ruinas in Aguadilla will captivate you as the sky transforms from powder blue into a sea of reds, oranges, pinks, and purples.

## TIP

You can drive from east to west along the southern or northern coasts, or you can weave your way along the sinuous Ruta Panorámica that runs through the center of the island (see page 83). Depending on which route you choose, the drive can take between three and seven hours, giving you plenty of time to stop to sightsee along the way.

46

# GET SHIPWRECKED (NOT REALLY)

## ON GUILLIGAN'S ISLAND

Just sit right back and you'll hear a tale . . . of an offshore cay where you can spend the day snorkeling, kayaking, and playing in the Caribbean Sea. This mangrove-laden island near Guánica goes by many names—Cayo Aurora, Guilligan's Island, Gilligan's Island—but whatever you call it, it's the perfect place to set out for a three-hour (more or less …) tour. The water is so clear and calm that you don't even need to snorkel to see schools of fish fluttering about, but do yourself a favor and bring your gear to get a closer look at the starfish, pufferfish, and other tropical species that inhabit these waters. You can make the one-mile trip by kayak or board a small passenger ferry that shuttles guests back and forth from San Jacinto Restaurant in Guánica.

PR-333 km 6.8, Bo. Carenero, Guánica
787-821-4941

**TIP**

You can bring food with you, but fishing rods, glass bottles, pets, hammocks, and speakers are not allowed. And, of course, take all your trash with you when you leave.

47

# SWING LIKE TARZAN
## AT GOZALANDIA FALLS

Some people know them as El Roble (their official title), some call them Las Cascadas (Spanish for "the waterfalls"), and still others say Gozalandia, but no matter what name you use, you'll find natural beauty and adventure at these two exquisite waterfalls in San Sebastián. The lower falls are magnificent to behold, and if you're a thrill seeker, you won't be able to resist climbing to the top and propelling yourself into the natural pool at the bottom. Not feeling so daring? Wade in on foot to join the fun. A short walk away at the upper falls, a rope swing makes it easy to channel your inner Tarzan before plunging into the crisp, cool water.

Carr. 446 km 1.6, San Sebastián

**TIP**

While the attraction is located on public land, you can only access it via private property, where you can park for a small fee and enjoy natural fruit juices, frozen cocktails, and tasty bar food at the on-site café.

48

# JUMP OFF THE PIER
## AT CRASH BOAT BEACH

You'd better arrive early if you want to stake out a good spot on Crash Boat Beach on a Saturday or Sunday. This golden, sandy expanse in Aguadilla is one of the area's most popular hangouts, and for good reason. Palm trees provide shade if you want it, the water is as clear as a bathtub, and food shacks serve cold drinks and snacks. The area was once used as a fueling station for the US Navy, and the cement piers where the ships docked still jut out into the ocean. Jumping off the farthest, highest piling has become a rite of passage for kids and adults, who line up together to get their chance—and then get back in line to do it all over again.

PR-458, Aguadilla

**TIP**

Crash Boat is also known for its stellar snorkeling and scuba diving, as fish come to eat the algae that grows on the pier's pylons.

49

# PLANT TREES
## FOR PUERTO RICO'S FUTURE

Trees are vital to sustaining life, but when Hurricanes Irma and Maria tore through Puerto Rico in September 2017, their brutal force wreaked havoc on the island's tree population. In the wake of the storms, Para la Naturaleza, a private nonprofit organization dedicated to preserving the local ecology, amped up its reforestation efforts, setting a goal to plant 750,000 endemic and native trees by 2026. At sites across the island, you can do your part to help fulfill this important mission. Sign up online for a myriad of volunteer opportunities, like finding and collecting seeds, maintaining nurseries, and planting trees in protected areas. You'll have a great time getting your hands dirty and knowing that you're helping ensure a bright and sustainable future for Puerto Rico.

787-722-5882
paralanaturaleza.org

### TIP

Para la Naturaleza oversees many volunteer projects that protect Puerto Rico's natural habitats and preserve its history. You can participate in everything from harvesting iguana eggs and identifying birds to helping with coastal cleanups and archaeological digs.

50

# BEACH HOP
## IN MANATÍ

Three of Puerto Rico's most distinctive beaches dot the northern coast in Manatí, and you can visit them all in one salty, sandy day. Start at Mar Chiquita, where you can watch the fierce waves of the Atlantic break angrily against the rocks while you splash around in a horseshoe-shaped cove. Next, drive ten minutes west, park the car on the side of the road, and follow the path to the right to reach Poza de Mujeres, a wide stretch of beach with jagged rocks and foamy surf. The trail to the left takes you through the brush to Cueva de las Golondrinas, named for the cave-like overhang where swallows return to nest at sunset, making it the perfect place to end your day.

Tierras Nuevas Poniente, Manatí

### TIP

Food kiosks set up shop in the parking lot at Mar Chiquita on the weekends.

51

# RIDE A PASO FINO HORSE
## ON PLAYA NEGRA

Horses roam freely on the rustic island of Vieques. You'll see them running along the roads, playing on the beach, and grazing in herds in the open fields. But these aren't your average equines. They are Paso Finos, a breed whose rhythmic gait creates a notably smooth ride that you can experience for yourself on a tour with Esperanza Riding Company. Settle into the saddle for a relaxing two-hour ride, during which you'll explore parts of the island that you can't reach by car. The trip goes from enjoyable to extraordinary when you turn the corner onto Playa Negra. As your horse frolics through the surf on this striking black-sand beach, you'll feel as if you stepped out of a painting that's so stunning, it can't be real. But it is.

787-435-0073
esperanzaridingcompany.com/vieques

### TIP

Esperanza Riding Company takes groups out in the early morning or late afternoon to avoid the hottest part of the day. Space is limited, so book in advance to secure your spot.

# SCUBA DIVE
## THE PUERTO RICAN TRENCH

If you're serious about scuba, then you'll find your underwater paradise at the Puerto Rican Trench. This unique formation, also called the Wall, marks the intersection of the Atlantic Ocean and the Caribbean Sea, creating a dramatic vertical wall where the sea floor drops from levels of 50 feet to 80 feet to 130 feet and so on, all the way down to more than 1,000 feet. You'll be mesmerized by the plethora of colorful sea creatures that swim in these high-visibility waters, from moray eels and pufferfish to Puerto Rican reef sharks and sea turtles. The trench features more than forty buoyed dive sites, and several PADI-approved operators run trips that typically depart from Guánica, where it's only a twelve-minute boat ride to the closest buoy, or from La Parguera in Lajas.

Island Scuba, Playa Santa
Carr. 325 Final, Bo. Ensenada, Guánica
787-309-6556
sanjuandiver.com

Paradise Scuba & Snorkeling
Carr. 304, km 3.2, La Parguera, Lajas
787-899-7611
paradisescubasnorkelingpr.com

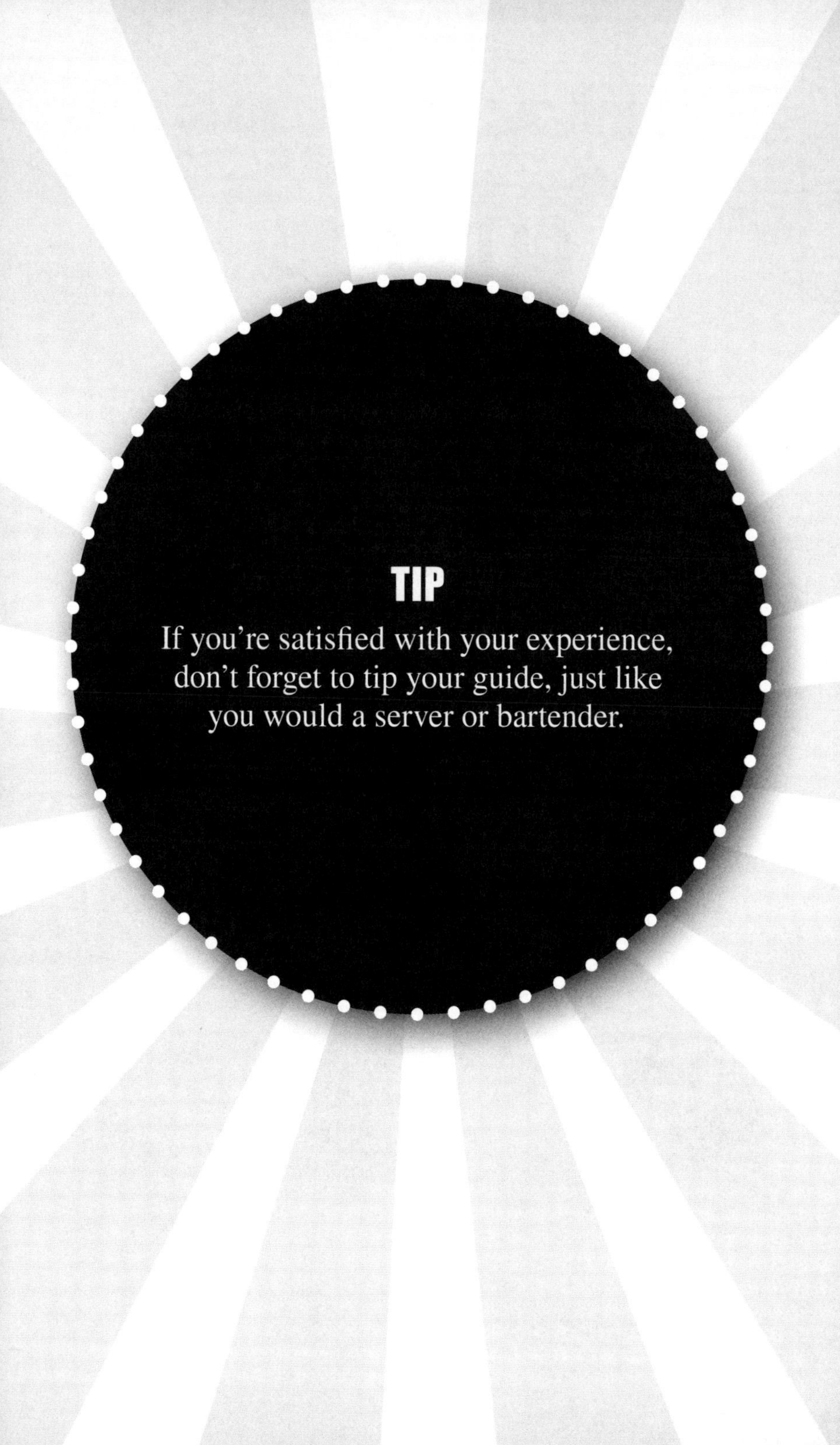

## TIP

If you're satisfied with your experience, don't forget to tip your guide, just like you would a server or bartender.

53

# GET LIFTED
## IN EL GLOBO

You can't leave Jayuya without taking a spin in El Globo, Puerto Rico's first aerostatic balloon. Located on a hilltop 3,200 feet above sea level, the helium-filled attraction looks like a hot air balloon, but instead of flying through the air, it moves up and down while tethered to the ground. The one-hundred-foot-tall, brightly colored balloon is easy to spot from afar, but its eye-catching design isn't just for decoration. Red and green are Jayuya's official colors, and the image of a petroglyph represents the area's importance to the Taíno culture. El Globo holds as many as twenty-eight passengers, and once you climb aboard, you'll ascend another five hundred feet and take in 360-degree views of the hills and valleys around you.

Carr. 530 km 0.2, Bo. Mamayes, Jayuya
787-828-0900
facebook.com/globoaerostaticojayuya

### TIP

Riding in El Globo is weather dependent, so if it's too rainy, foggy, or windy, the balloon stays grounded.

54

# BIRDWATCH
## IN THE GUÁNICA STATE FOREST

Designated a United Nations Biosphere Reserve for its high ecological value, the Guánica State Forest in southwest Puerto Rico presents one of the Caribbean's most noteworthy natural habitats. The nine-thousand-acre coastal dry forest only gets about thirty-five inches of rain each year (compared to more than fifteen feet in El Yunque), creating conditions in which hundreds of species of flora and fauna thrive. Birders particularly love it here, as the area is home to at least 130 types of avians, more than anywhere else on the island. The Department of Natural and Environmental Resources oversees the site, and you can pick up a map at the welcome center, where park rangers are happy to offer advice about navigating the forest's twelve hiking trails.

Carr. 334, Guánica
787-724-3724

**TIP**

Many trees here drop their leaves during dry season between December and April and reflower between August and November when the weather is wetter.

55

# JUMP OUT OF A PLANE
## FROM TEN THOUSAND FEET

What's the best way to get a birds-eye view of Puerto Rico? By jumping out of an airplane, of course. The team at Xtreme Divers in Arecibo is ready to show you the beauty of the island from above on an unforgettable skydiving adventure. After a Cessna carries you up to an altitude of ten thousand feet, you'll plummet in freefall at 120 miles per hour. Once your parachute opens, you'll float safely to the ground while gazing in wonder at vast ocean waters, white-sand beaches, and majestic mountains. If you're new to skydiving, don't worry, you'll jump in tandem tethered to a trained professional. Owner Jason Gonzales has more than twenty thousand jumps under his belt, so you know you're in good hands.

Aeropuerto Antonio (Nery) Juarbe, Arecibo
787-852-5757
xtremedivers.com

### TIP

The annual Free Fall Festival in February draws hundreds of skydivers to the area for five days of jumping, partying, and adrenaline-fueled fun.

56

# SEE LEATHERBACK TURTLES NEST
## AND HATCH IN DORADO

Clocking in at more than 1,500 pounds, leatherback sea turtles are the planet's largest turtles, and the archipelago of Puerto Rico is a haven for the endangered species. Chelonia, a private nonprofit organization, works to protect and study these marine reptiles, and if you're curious to learn more, you can tag along while the scientists do their firsthand research. Join the group on select nights in April and May as they troll for nests on Dorado Beach, where as many as four hundred turtles lay their eggs each year. Then in July, witness the miracle of life when the eggs hatch and the newborns crawl to the water. You'll help measure, count, and mark each one, leaving you with an indelible memory and a new appreciation for leatherbacks.

facebook.com/cheloniapr

**TIP**

Be prepared to spend hours and walk for miles looking for nesting turtles. Hatching excursions are much less rigorous, since Chelonia already knows where to find each nest.

Túnel de Guajataca
(Photo Credit: Victor M. Velázquez / Evo Photography)

Jobos Beach, Isabela
(Photo Credit: Ran Rivera @ran_dee2)

Gozalandia Falls
(Photo Credit: Jonathan Veguilla @amazing787)

Finca El Girasol
(Photo Credit: Bianca Lives Local)

El Globo
(Photo Credit: Amy Gordon)

Arecibo Observatory
(Photo Credit: Courtesy of the Arecibo Observatory, a facility of the National Science Foundation)

Hawksbill Turtle
(Photo Credit: Sarah Elise P Field, Crystal Clear LLC)

Las Salinas de Cabo Rojo
(Photo Credit: Jonathan Veguilla @amazing787)

Old San Juan
(Photo Credit: Amy Gordon)

Isla de Mona
(Photo Credit: José Márquez)

Río Tanamá
(Photo Credit: Rosario Fernández Esteve)

Vieques
(Photo Credit: Elliott Anderson)

Surfing in Rincón
(Photo Credit: racheltannerphotography.com)

Parque de Bombas
(Photo Credit: Ran Rivera @ran_dee2)

Icacos
(Photo Credit: Victor M. Velázquez / Evo Photography)

The Puerto Rican Flag
(Photo Credit: Anthony F. Cozzolino)

Yauco
(Photo Credit: Ran Rivers@ran_dee2)

Shopping in Old San Juan
(Photo Credit: Amy Gordon)

57

# CAMP OUT
## ON PLAYA FLAMENCO

It only takes one glimpse of Playa Flamenco to understand why this sundrenched expanse on the north coast of Culebra consistently ranks as one of the world's most beautiful beaches. The sand is so white and the water so clear that you can barely make out where the ocean meets the shore, and you won't be able to stop yourself from jumping in. A palm-treed perimeter separates the beach from a smattering of kiosks that sell everything you need for a carefree day, from pinchos and fruit smoothies to sunscreen and ice. But your time on Flamenco doesn't have to end when the sun goes down. Camper-friendly amenities like bathrooms, outdoor showers, and a potable water station make it easy to spend the night.

Carr. 251, Culebra

**TIP**

To secure a camping permit, contact the Department of Natural and Environmental Resources (DRNA) at 787-742-0700 or register on-site at the Flamenco Campground Office.

58

# OBSERVE THE PRIMATES
## ON MONKEY ISLAND

An island ruled by monkeys sounds like science fiction, but on Cayo Santiago, it's very real. This thirty-eight-acre cay off the coast of Humacao was founded as a research facility in 1938, when scientists brought roughly four hundred rhesus macaques from India to Puerto Rico. Today, "Monkey Island" continues to be an invaluable resource to researchers from all over the world, offering a rare opportunity to observe the animals in an isolated environment to learn about tropical diseases, brain disorders, and group behavior. Only authorized personnel are allowed on the island, but you can watch the primates from the water either in your own boat or on a guided tour with Barefoot Travelers.

Barefoot Travelers Kayak Tour to Monkey Island
787-850-0508
barefoottravelersrooms.com/adventures.php

**TIP**

If you're tempted to break the rules and explore Cayo Santiago on foot, don't do it. The restrictions are in place to protect both the humans and the monkeys, each of whom carry diseases that can be deadly to the other.

59

# CAPTAIN YOUR OWN BOAT
## TO ICACOS

You can spot the islets of Palominos, Cayo Lobos, and Icacos from the coast of Fajardo, but why stop there? Travel by sea to see the beauty of these uninhabited islands up close. Several tour operators offer party boat excursions where you can spend the day drinking and soaking in the sun, or you can go over in a water taxi. But for a more exciting experience, book a guided tour in a mini-motorboat with Kayaking Puerto Rico. You'll feel the thrill that comes with captaining your own vessel—no license required. After you and your group snorkel a vibrant coral reef, you'll pull up to the beach and spend some time on Icacos, an unspoiled cay where the sand is as powdery soft as the water is crystal clear.

Marina Puerto Chico, Fajardo
787-245-4545
kayakingpuertorico.com

**TIP**

The salty spray of the ocean isn't kind to electronic devices. If you have an item you want to keep dry, leave it locked up at the dock.

60

# NAVIGATE THE TWISTS AND TURNS OF LA RUTA PANORÁMICA

Your journey along La Ruta Panorámica is sure to be one of the most memorable drives of your life, because of both its treacherous terrain and its jaw-dropping scenery. This 167-mile route weaves its way through the Cordillera Central mountain range, where surprises linger at every turn. Dense plant life might surround you one minute, only to open up onto sweeping views of mountains, valleys, farms, and rivers the next. You'll be white knuckled on narrow inclines before cruising along smooth, flat stretches. After driving for miles without seeing a soul, you'll come upon quaint towns where you can pull over and grab a bite. And while you can drive the entire length in roughly seven hours, traversing even a portion of it makes for an unforgettable adventure.

**TIP**

Don't be intimidated into speeding up if you see a line of cars behind you. Exercising caution is much more important than driving fast.

# HIT THE LINKS
## ON THE NORTHWEST COAST

Duffers are in for a treat on the northwest coast of Puerto Rico, where two courses look out onto scenery so beautiful that you might have a hard time keeping your eye on the ball. You can see the ocean from every hole at Aguadilla's Punta Borinquen Golf Club, which was originally built as a recreational outlet for the US military. In fact, President Eisenhower even played a round here. When the base closed in 1973, the course became the island's first municipal golf club. Thirteen miles to the east at the tony Royal Isabela resort, the contours of the natural landscape dictate the design of the renowned course, and the greens abut cliffs that drop two hundred feet into the Atlantic Ocean.

Punta Borinquen Golf Club
300 Golf Road, Ramey Base, Aguadilla
787-890-2987
puntaborinquengolfclub.org

Royal Isabela
300 Ave. Noel Estrada, Isabela
787-609-5888
royalisabela.com/golf

### TIP

Puerto Rico's first golf course opened in 1911 on the lawn at El Morro in Old San Juan. It remained operational until 1966.

# KEEP AN EYE OUT FOR MANATEES
## AT PLAYA SUCIA

Mother Nature carved out a piece of perfection at La Playuela in Cabo Rojo. Locals call this tucked-away treasure Playa Sucia (Dirty Beach), but don't let the nickname fool you. The pristine white sand is powder soft, the warm water spans every shade of blue, and you might even spot a manatee or two playing in the near distance. You can take a short hike up to Faro Los Morrillos lighthouse to view the crescent-shaped shoreline from above, explore the surrounding limestone formations for hidden caves and a natural rock bridge, cool off in the water, or simply relax under an umbrella with a book in hand. Whatever type of day at the beach you're looking for, you'll find it here.

Carr. 301, Cabo Rojo

### TIP

The road that leads to this beach is unpaved and rocky, so be prepared for a (manageably) bumpy ride.

63

# GET A MASSAGE IN A TREEHOUSE
## AT SPA BOTÁNICO

Picture it: you're lying on a plush massage table high in the trees. As a pair of healing hands works to relieve your every stress, a soft breeze sweeps over you, carrying with it the sweet scent of the pineapple garden below. If you think that this blissful scenario sounds too good to be true, then you haven't been to Spa Botánico, a five-acre oasis of calm at the uber-luxurious Dorado Beach, a Ritz-Carlton Reserve. Treatments begin with a visit to the apothecary, where you'll select a blend of aromatic botanicals and essential oils before ascending to an open-air massage room built into the branches of tropical trees. The only downside? Your time here might ruin other spas for you forever.

100 Dorado Beach Dr., Dorado
787-278-7227
ritzcarlton.com/en/hotels/puerto-rico/dorado-beach/spa

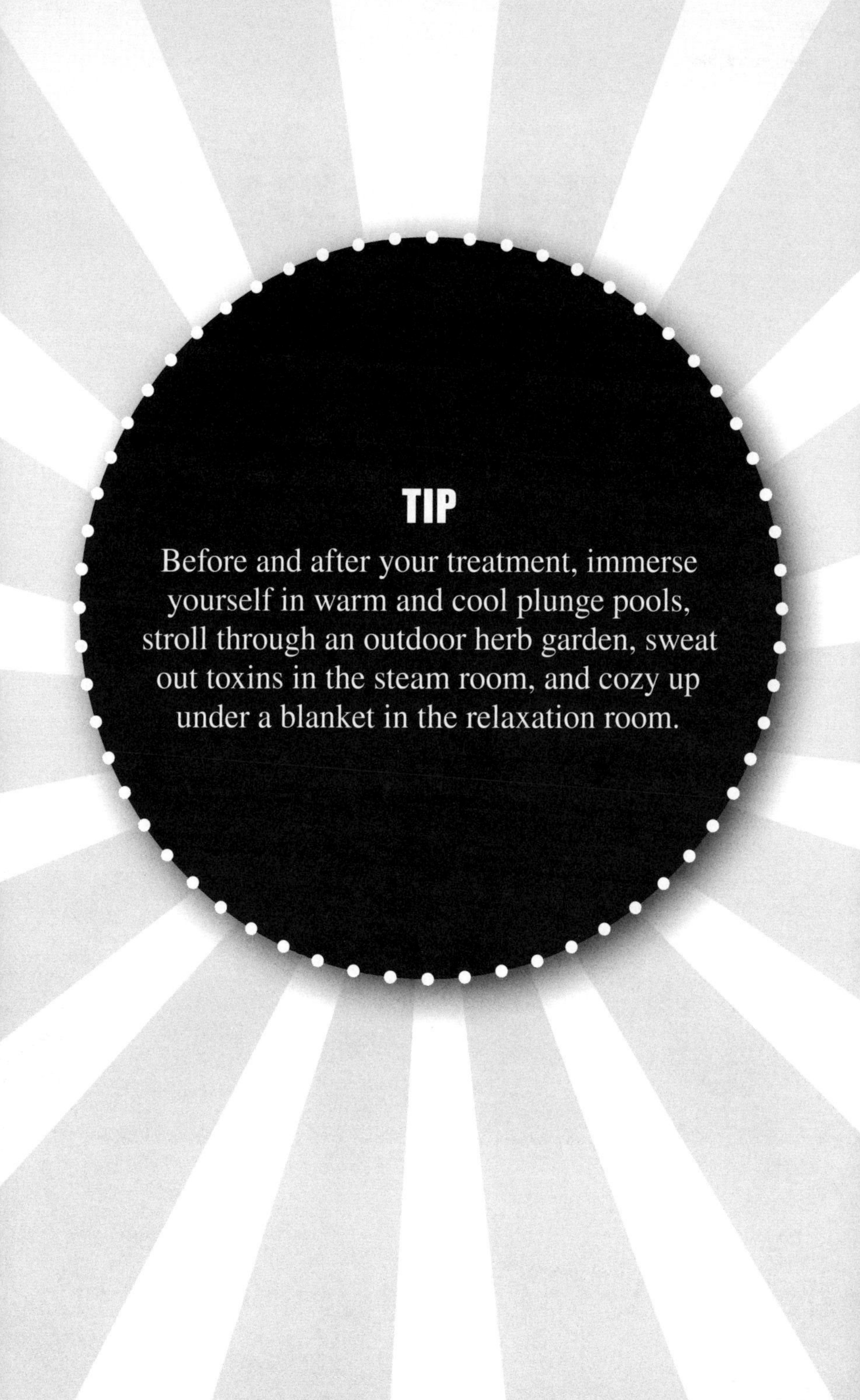
TIP
Before and after your treatment, immerse yourself in warm and cool plunge pools, stroll through an outdoor herb garden, sweat out toxins in the steam room, and cozy up under a blanket in the relaxation room.

64

# WALK TO THE BEACH
## THROUGH AN ABANDONED RAILROAD TUNNEL

In the late nineteenth and early twentieth centuries, a robust railroad system traversed the island of Puerto Rico, transporting sugar cane from farms to mills and ports. The train shut down in 1953 with the demise of the sugar industry, though remnants, like the Túnel de Guajataca (Guajataca Tunnel) that connected the municipalities of Isabela and Quebradillas, remain. The tracks have been replaced with pavement, creating a dramatic, pedestrian-friendly corridor that you can easily navigate in flip flops. Once you walk through the tunnel, a flat trail runs parallel to the ocean and leads you right to a lovely secluded beach, where golden sand, massive boulders, and foamy surf await.

Avenida Noel Estrada, Isabela

**TIP**

You might be tempted to take a dip in the ocean, but the waves here are fierce, and swimming is not recommended.

# CHOOSE YOUR ADVENTURE
## AT LA PARGUERA

Do you want to get into the water for some world-class scuba diving and snorkeling? Care to kayak through a forest of mangroves? In the mood to reel in a marlin or hook a tarpon? You can do it all at the waterside village of La Parguera in Lajas, where the boardwalk-style marina is lined with dive shops, tour companies, and charter boat operators. Prefer relaxation to adventure? Spend the day on the beach at one of the uninhabited cays that sit just offshore. The excitement continues after sundown, when you can splash in a bioluminescent bay and sip tropical cocktails at a string of bars before heading home.

Avenida Los Pescadores, Lajas

### TIP

Just over a mile east of La Parguera, you can go for a swim at Playa Rosada, the largest man-made natural pool in the Caribbean.

66

# GET SALTY
## IN CABO ROJO

The shallow lagoons of Las Salinas de Cabo Rojo (the Cabo Rojo Salt Flats, also called the Corozo Salt Flats) have been a reliable salt source for more than five hundred years. While the flats are still actively used for commercial salt production, they double as a fascinating tourist attraction. You can learn more about the site and its history at the Interpretive Center on the side of the road, which features educational materials and an informative video presentation. The building is only staffed Friday through Sunday, but you can walk among the towering mounds of crystals that sit outside any day of the week. If the three-story observation tower is open, be sure to climb to the top for a bird's-eye view of the pastel-colored aquatic surroundings.

Carr. 301 km 11, Cabo Rojo
787-851-2999

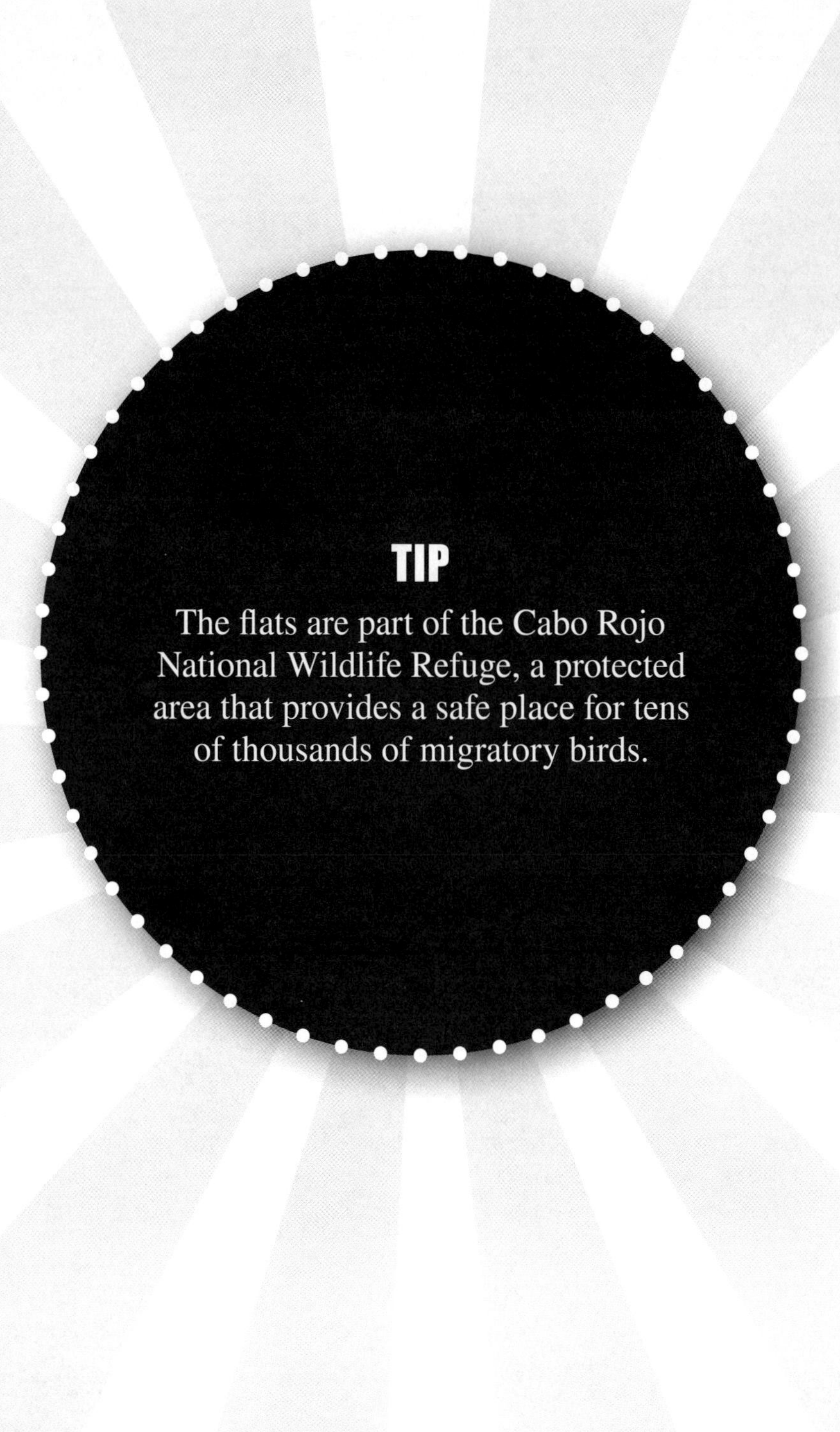

## TIP

The flats are part of the Cabo Rojo National Wildlife Refuge, a protected area that provides a safe place for tens of thousands of migratory birds.

67

# FLY A PLANE (WITHOUT A PILOT'S LICENSE!) OVER ARECIBO

If you've always wanted to fly a plane but don't have your pilot's license, Arecibo Light Sport Aviation can make your dream come true in a light sport aircraft. This two-passenger open-air vehicle looks like a cross between a go-kart and a hang glider, and it's even more fun to ride in than it is to see. After owner Jose Torres brings the plane to an altitude of between six hundred and one thousand feet, he'll hand over the reins to you, and you'll be in control as you soar over the northern coast. With no walls, windshield, or floor separating you from the elements, the views of Puerto Rico on one side and the Atlantic Ocean on the other are almost as thrilling as the rush you'll get from being a (temporary) pilot.

Aeropuerto Antonio (Nery) Juarbe, Arecibo
787-903-1725

### TIP

If your voyage inspires you to get your pilot's license, the company offers instruction and training to get you there.

# SPLASH AROUND IN NATURE'S WATERPARK
## AT LAS PAYLAS

For the fun of a waterpark without the price tag, long lines, and overly chlorinated pools, find your way to Las Paylas, a natural waterslide in Luquillo. This off-the-beaten-path attraction is literally in the surrounding homes' backyards, and you won't find any road signs pointing the way. You'll know you've arrived when you spot a trash bin painted with "Las Paylas" in front of a neighboring house, where you can park for a small fee. The slides are busy with kids and adults on weekends, so watch their technique for pointers, tuck your elbows, and let the current propel you on a fast-moving thrill ride into the pool below. Once you've made it to the bottom, you won't be able to keep yourself from climbing back up to do it again . . . and again . . . and again.

Carr. 983, Bo. Los Ramos, Luquillo

### TIP

The river can get rough after periods of heavy rain, and there's no lifeguard on duty, so proceed with caution.

# CRAWL THROUGH A CAVE
## AT LAS CABACHUELAS

For a day of excitement and exploration, set out on a spelunking trip to Las Cabachuelas de Morovis. This intricate network of more than sixty caverns in Puerto Rico's karst region holds tremendous archaeological and scientific value. Inside, you'll find dark tunnels and speleothem-laden spaces where you can spot ancient petroglyphs and fossils, as well as plants and animals that thrive in lightless environments. A handful of the caves are open to visitors, but you can only access them through private property. To avoid trespassing, book a tour with a licensed operator like Borikua Tours or CABACOOP. Their knowledgeable guides will provide all the gear and expertise you need.

Borikua Tours
787-403-5581
borikuatourspr.com

CABACOOP
facebook.com/CentroCulturalDeMorovis

## TIP

You'll crawl through small passageways when you explore the caves, so be prepared for some tight squeezes.

La Perla Cemetery
(Photo Credit: Victor M. Velázquez / Evo Photography)

# CULTURE AND HISTORY

# FLY A KITE
## AT EL MORRO

With walls that tower 140 feet high, Castillo San Felipe del Morro—commonly known as El Morro—has guarded San Juan Bay for nearly four hundred years. The fort was built to last by the Spanish to protect Puerto Rico from attacks by sea, and it remained an active (US) military base through World War II. Today, the UNESCO World Heritage Site is one of the island's most trafficked tourist attractions, and the expansive lawn that stretches between the fort and the city is often packed with families picnicking on the grass and launching kites. Look up and you'll see a vast sky filled with colorful flyers in all shapes and sizes. Then grab your own and watch it soar, carried by the winds coming off the bay.

501 Calle Norzagaray, Adjuntas, Old San Juan
nps.gov/saju

### TIP

About a mile east of El Morro, Castillo San Cristóbal was built to guard the city from invasion by land. Like its neighbor, the twenty-seven-acre site is now a museum that's open to the public.

# STEP BACK IN TIME
## IN SAN GERMÁN

The most famous monument in San Germán, Puerto Rico's second-oldest city, is Porta Coeli, Puerto Rico's second-oldest church, but there is so much more to explore here. The Museo de la Historia de San Germán is a great place to start. What was once a savings and loan now displays items that highlight the town's heritage, from banking to basketball. The friendly staff are happy to direct you to other points of interest, like the Museo Farmacia La Botica, the Museo de Arte y Casa Estudio, and the ornate Iglesia San Germán de Auxerre church. In between sightseeing stops, meander along the cobblestone streets and admire the neoclassical architecture that secured the entire Historic District a slot on the National Register of Historic Places.

Museo de la Historia de San Germán
32 Calle Dr. Veve, San Germán
787-892-3670
mhisapr.org

Porta Coeli
Plaza Porta Coeli, San Germán

**TIP**

For a picture-perfect vantage point of Porta Coeli, enjoy tacos and margaritas on the outdoor patio at Lupito's Mexican restaurant across the street.

# BE PART OF THE SOLUTION
## AT CASA PUEBLO

When a massive mining operation threatened to destroy thirty-six thousand acres of wilderness in the center of Puerto Rico, a group of determined activists fought back, ultimately saving the area from ecological disaster. Their unlikely success sparked them to formally establish Casa Pueblo, a community-based organization that has affected social, political, and environmental change for more than three decades. You'll be both humbled and inspired when you visit Casa Pueblo's Adjuntas headquarters, where you can learn about the organization's myriad endeavors, like its working coffee plantation, clean energy initiatives, butterfly garden, solar-powered movie theater, and music school for kids. But more than the sum of its projects, Casa Pueblo is a dynamic example of the power of the collective community spirit.

30 Calle Rodulfo González, Adjuntas
787-829-4842, casapueblo.org

### TIP

Casa Pueblo still oversees a portion of the land it originally saved, now called Bosque del Pueblo. Closer to town at Bosque Escuela (School Forest), visitors can enjoy the outdoors and learn about biodiversity in a natural environment.

73

# WALK BACKWARDS INTO THE OCEAN

## ON NOCHE DE SAN JUAN

Christians all over the world observe the Feast of St. John the Baptist on June 24, but in Puerto Rico, the celebration begins after the sun goes down on June 23. To be a part of a local rite of passage, head to the nearest beach, where you'll likely see family and friends gathering for a high-spirited evening filled with delicious food and drinks, music, and a unique island tradition. As midnight approaches, the crowd heads for the ocean and joins hands facing the shore. The countdown begins, and when the clock strikes twelve, everyone walks backwards into the waves and submerges under the water in a baptism of sorts, clearing the way for good luck in the coming year.

**TIP**

There's no hard-and-fast rule for the number of times you're supposed to dip under the water. Some say three, others say seven, and still others dunk twelve times.

# TOUR THE HOUSE THAT DON Q BUILT

## AT CASTILLO SERRALLÉS

High on a hilltop overlooking Ponce sits Castillo Serrallés, a sprawling estate that originally belonged to Don Juan Eugenio Serrallés, the tycoon behind Don Q rum. Built in the 1930s, the stately mansion remained in the family for generations until the City of Ponce purchased it and opened it to the public as a museum in 1991. Today, Castillo Serrallés is an impeccably preserved example of Spanish Revival architecture, complete with most of the home's original furniture, artwork, and fixtures. Guided tours begin with a short video, and from there an expert leads you through rooms that are staged as they would have been in the mansion's heyday. Through the legacy of one prominent family, Castillo Serrallés sheds light on an opulent era of Puerto Rico's past.

El Vigía #17 Final, Ponce
787-259-1775
museocastilloserralles.com

### TIP

Adjacent to the castle, the towering Cruceta de Vigía looks like a giant religious symbol, but it was actually built to spot incoming ships. Climb the 102 steps to the vantage point to take in sweeping views of the Caribbean Sea.

75

# HANG OUT WHERE THE TAÍNOS DID
## AT LA PIEDRA ESCRITA

For hundreds of years before Christopher Columbus arrived, the island was inhabited by an indigenous race known as the Taínos. Today, La Piedra Escrita (the Written Stone), which sits on a shallow riverbed of the Río Saliente in Jayuya, offers a glimpse into what life was like here so many centuries ago. Dwarfing the rocks that surround it, the stone is striking to see, and its smooth surface makes it easy to identify the spirals, faces, and other petroglyph symbols that the Taínos used to communicate with their gods. Its historical importance is profound, and if you touch the stone and close your eyes, you almost expect to find yourself transported back in time when you open them.

Carr. 144 km 7.3, Bo. Coabey, Jayuya

### TIP

What was once a visitor center now sits empty, but the parking lot is open and the wooden boardwalk that leads down to the river is well maintained.

# STUMBLE UPON THE REMAINS

## OF THE PLAYA GRANDE SUGAR MILL

Entering the Playa Grande Sugar Mill Ruins on Vieques feels like walking onto the set of *Lost*. As you make your way through the lush jungle, thick vines drape heavily over broken brick buildings, underground tunnels lead you down hidden passageways, and you might stumble upon a rusty train car turned on its side, even though there are no railroad tracks in sight. While this overgrown forest is now an intriguing place to explore, in the nineteenth and early twentieth centuries it was a hub of the island's then-thriving sugar industry. Production ceased once the US Navy built a base on Vieques in the 1940s, but the area remains a can't-miss spot for curious adventurers.

Playa Grande Sugar Mill Ruins
Bo. Playa Grande, Vieques

Vieques Conservation & Historical Trust
138 Calle Flamboyán, Bo. Esperanza, Vieques
787-741-8850
vcht.org

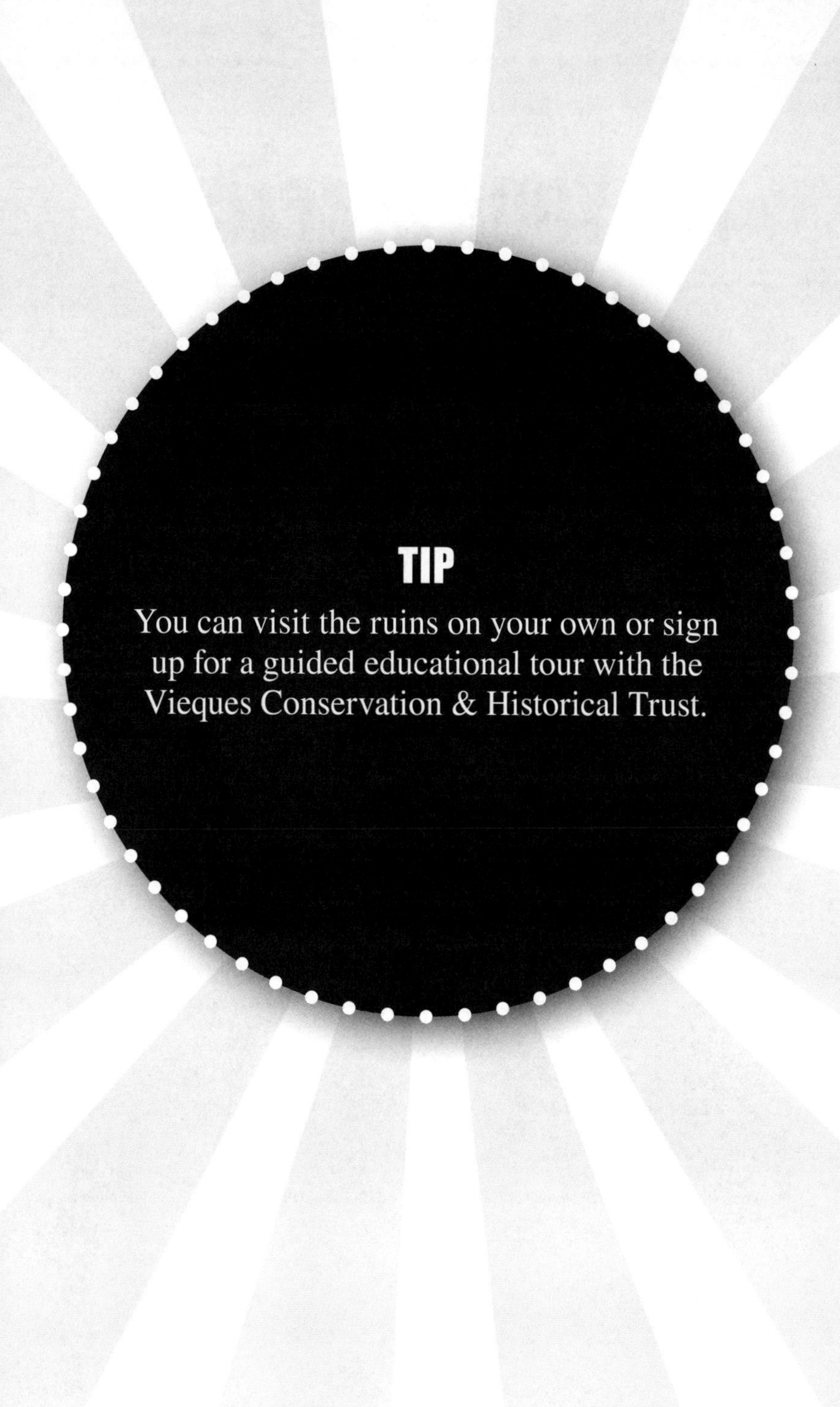
TIP
You can visit the ruins on your own or sign up for a guided educational tour with the Vieques Conservation & Historical Trust.

77

# PAY YOUR RESPECTS
## AT LA PERLA CEMETERY

Cementerio Santa María Magdalena de Pazzis (also known as La Perla Cemetery or the Old San Juan Cemetery) is one of the most iconic sites in Puerto Rico's capital city. This bayside burial ground dates back to 1863 and serves as the final resting place for some of Puerto Rico's most prominent citizens, including Academy Award winner José Ferrer, educator Rafael Cordero, politician Lolita Lebrón, and comedian Ramón "Diplo" Rivera. You can get a photo-worthy perspective from above at El Morro, but seeing it from inside the forty-foot walls is a truly moving experience. The stone statues of saints draped in flowing robes, carved crosses laden with flowers, and intricate marble tombstones are both tributes to those who have passed on and beautiful works of art.

Calle Cementerio, Old San Juan

### TIP

Pedestrians and cars share the short tunnel that leads to the cemetery's main gate, so be careful when you pass through it.

78

# SEE HOW ART
## TRANSFORMED A TOWN IN YAUCO

Pito Hernández was enjoying a cup of coffee in his hometown of Yauco when he had an idea: if he could turn the staircase leading up the hill into an eye-catching work of art, people might be more likely to venture up to enjoy the view. In 2017, with the help of local students and the support of the municipality, Nuestra Bandera Yaucana was born. The project transformed the stairs—and many of the surrounding buildings—into a colorful expression of urban art, uniting the neighborhood in look and spirit, improving the quality of life for residents, and boosting the economy. Hernández later expanded the project and invited a select group of Puerto Rican artists to create murals all over town. Today, nearly five thousand people from around the world make their way to Yauco each week to see these masterpieces in person.

Yaucromatic
Yauco Pueblo, Yauco

**TIP**

Go to yaucromatic.com to learn more about the artists and access an interactive map that leads you to each mural.

# EXPERIENCE SIX ECOSYSTEMS IN ONE PLACE

## AT LAS CABEZAS DE SAN JUAN

If you think that Puerto Rico is all beaches and mountains, a visit to Las Cabezas de San Juan will enlighten you. Within its 450 acres, this fascinating nature reserve in Fajardo encompasses six distinct ecosystems: a bioluminescent lagoon, a mangrove forest, seagrass beds, sandy and rocky beaches, coral reefs, and a dry forest. Las Cabezas de San Juan is open to the public Wednesday through Sunday, but you can only explore on guided trolley tours administered by Para la Naturaleza, a nonprofit organization that oversees important natural and historical sites throughout Puerto Rico. Expert tour leaders offer insight into each biosphere, happily answer questions from the group, and are quick to point out exotic flora and fauna.

Carr. 987 km 5.9, Las Croabas, Fajardo
787-722-5882
paralanaturaleza.org/cabezas-de-san-juan

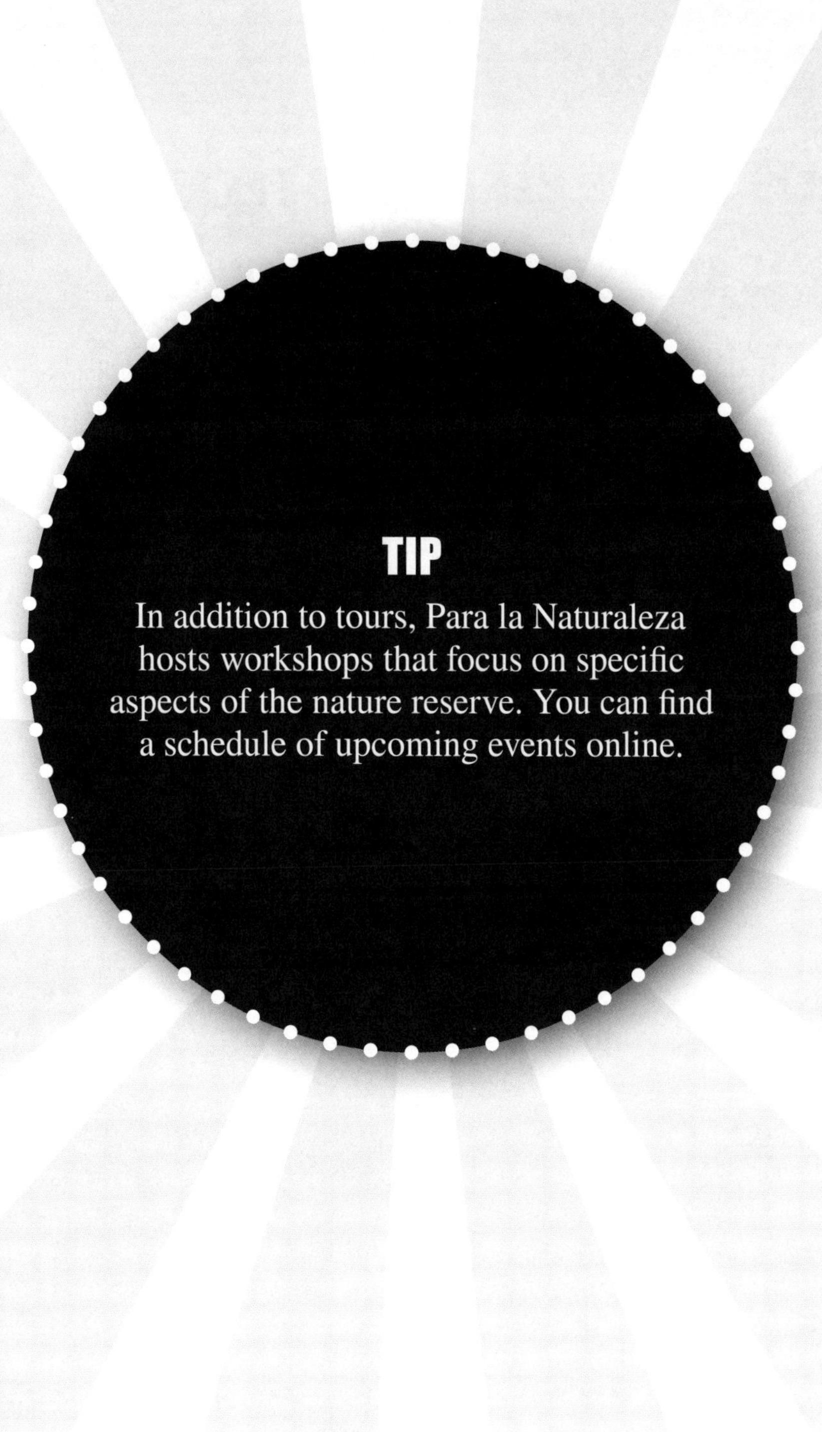

## TIP

In addition to tours, Para la Naturaleza hosts workshops that focus on specific aspects of the nature reserve. You can find a schedule of upcoming events online.

80

# LISTEN FOR ALIENS
## AT THE ARECIBO OBSERVATORY

In 1974, astronomers made their first attempt at communicating with extraterrestrials, and they did it from the Arecibo Observatory, home of the world's most powerful radio telescope. While we haven't received a response from outer space (yet), you never know when a message might make its way here—and who or what might send it. Completed in 1963, the telescope looks more like a giant satellite dish than a traditional optical telescope. The apparatus comprises nearly forty thousand aluminum panels and uses radio waves, rather than visual light, to magnify what's happening in the universe. You can visit the facility Wednesday through Sunday to view the technological marvel in person from the outdoor observation deck and learn from the interactive educational exhibits at the Science & Visitor Center.

Carr. 625, Bo. Esperanza, Arecibo
787-878-2612 Ext. 346
naic.edu/ao

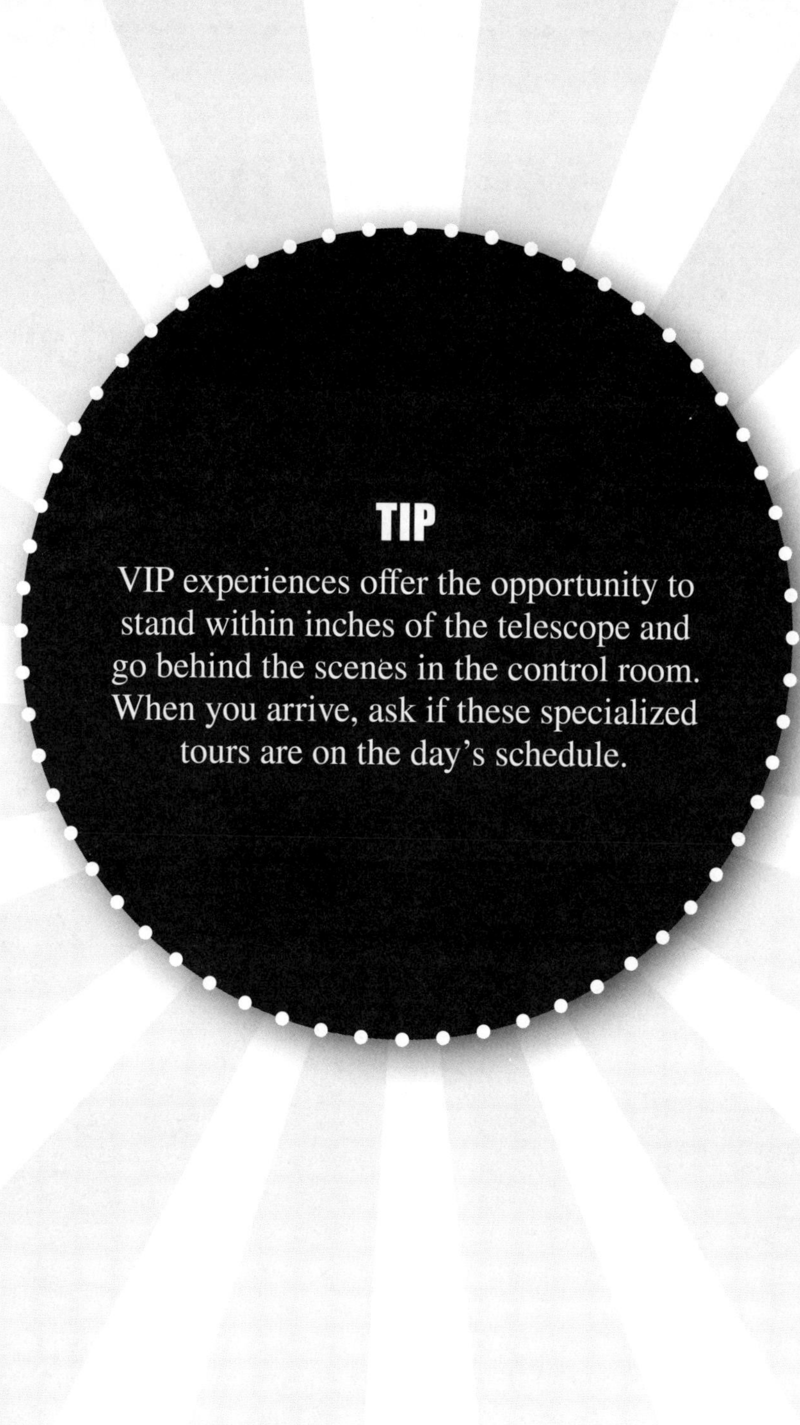

## TIP

VIP experiences offer the opportunity to stand within inches of the telescope and go behind the scenes in the control room. When you arrive, ask if these specialized tours are on the day's schedule.

## 81

# FIND SERENITY IN THE SCULPTURE GARDEN

## AT THE MUSEO DE ARTE DE PUERTO RICO

The Museo de Arte de Puerto Rico, which opened its doors in Santurce in 2000, comprises more than 1,200 works of art. Housed in a neoclassical building that once served as a municipal hospital, the museum encompasses twenty-four modern galleries where you can gaze upon original masterpieces from both prominent and up-and-coming Puerto Rican artists. After you've perused the galleries, step out the back door to see nature and art intertwine in the Sculpture Botanical Garden, a peaceful oasis from the busy neighborhood outside. In addition to sixteen site-specific sculptures, the 2.5-acre space features pergolas for quiet contemplation, twenty-six species of trees, 106,000 plants, and a tranquil koi pond dotted with lily pads, lagoons, and cascading waterfalls.

299 Avenida de Diego
Santurce, San Juan
787-977-6277
mapr.org

## TIP

Entry to the museum (which includes access to the Sculpture Botanical Garden) is free on Wednesdays from 2 to 8 p.m.

82

# SEE THE FOREST FOR THE TREES
## AT THE TROPICAL AGRICULTURE RESEARCH STATION

Horticulture enthusiasts find heaven on earth at the Tropical Agriculture Research Station (TARS) in Mayagüez, where the US Department of Agriculture actively studies more than two thousand species of plants, trees, and flowers. The 235-acre facility was established in 1902 through an appropriation from the US Congress to address agricultural issues that face Puerto Rico and the Caribbean, and it remains at the forefront of groundbreaking international research today. But TARS isn't just for scientists. The campus is open to the public on weekdays for self-guided tours. Grab a map at the information office and stroll the grounds at your own pace. You'll encounter hundreds of plots with plant life of all kinds. Each is marked with information about its species and its origins, so you'll know exactly what you're seeing.

2200 P.A. Campos Ave., Mayagüez
787-831-3435, ext. 0
ars.usda.gov/saa/tars

TIP
Rain showers are common in Mayagüez in the afternoon, so plan to visit TARS in the morning if you can.

# LEARN HOW WATER BECOMES POWER

## AT HACIENDA BUENA VISTA

Built in the 1840s when Puerto Rico was still under Spanish rule, Hacienda Buena Vista was more than just a coffee and chocolate plantation. Ponce's prominent Vives family, who owned the land, were technological pioneers who figured out how to harness the power of the mighty Río Canas river to run the farm's machinery. The property is now owned by the nonprofit organization Para la Naturaleza, and you can take a guided tour that chronicles this important intersection of nature and agriculture. You'll even see an original hydraulic turbine, the only one of its kind in the world. Prized for its natural beauty as well as its historical value, the 482-acre hacienda also includes a subtropical forest where you can swim under Salto Vives, a waterfall named for the farm's founders.

Carr. 123, km 17.3, Ponce
787-722-5882
paralanaturaleza.org/hacienda-buena-vista

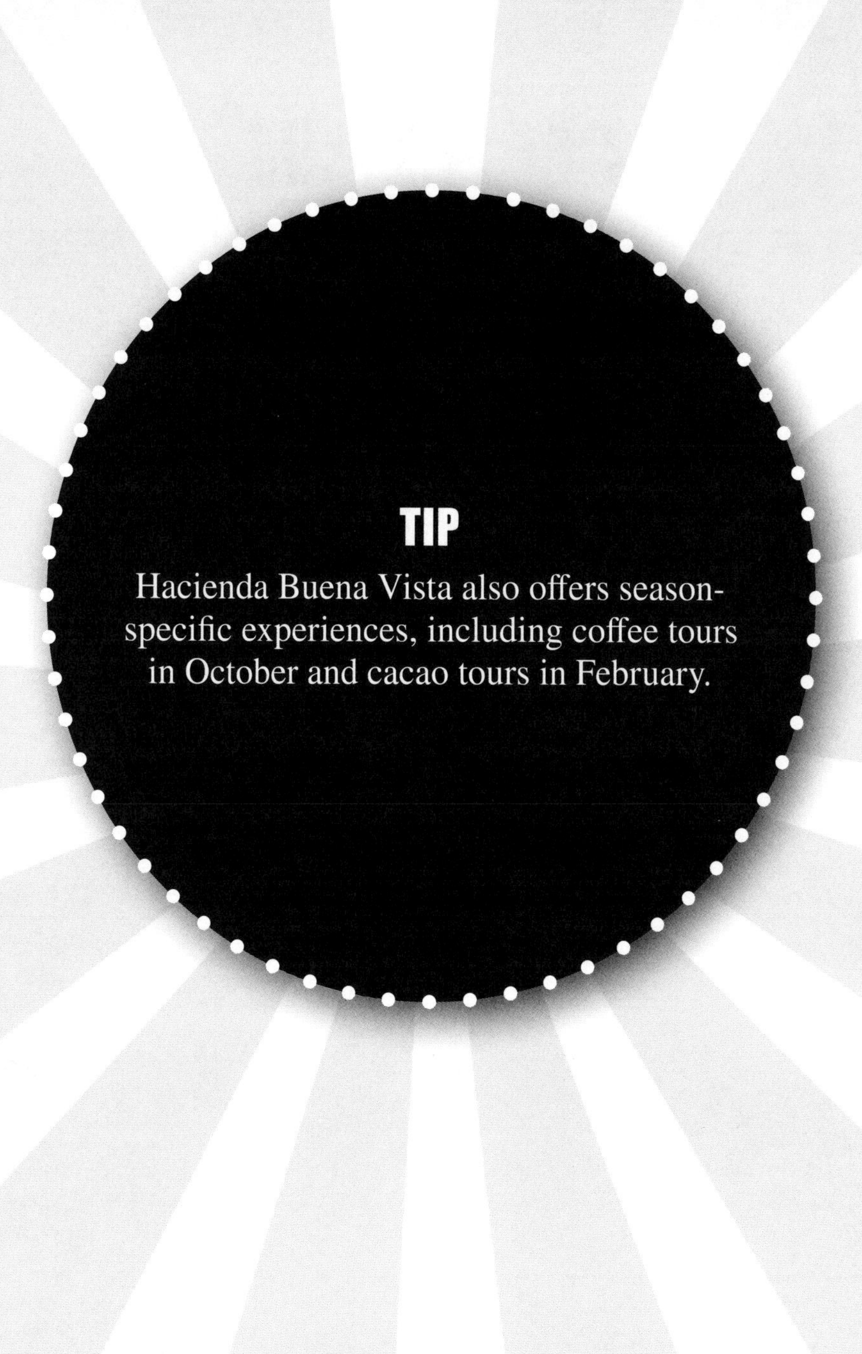

## TIP

Hacienda Buena Vista also offers season-specific experiences, including coffee tours in October and cacao tours in February.

# GET FESTIVE
## ALL YEAR LONG

You can always find a reason to celebrate in Puerto Rico. Seventy-eight municipalities make up the territory's three inhabited islands, and each hosts at least one festival every year where revelers rejoice with parades, food, drinks, music, art, and cultural programs. Some, like San Juan's culinary extravaganza Saborea Puerto Rico and the minty Mojito Fest, are modern, ticketed events, while others, like Hatillo's colorful Festival de las Máscaras (Mask Festival) and Carnaval Ponceño in Ponce, are free, fun-filled parties that honor different aspects of Puerto Rico's heritage. The events listed here are just a handful of the many fiestas where you can eat, drink, and be merry.

**January**
Festival de la Novilla (Heifer Festival), San Sebastián

**February**
Fiesta del Acabe del Café (Coffee Harvest Festival), Maricao

**March**
Festival de la China Dulce (Sweet Orange Festival), Las Marías

**April**
Festival del Maíz (Corn Festival), Canóvanas

**May**
Agroferia Nacional Coloso (Agricultural Festival), Aguada

**June**
Festival de la Piña Paradisíaca (Pineapple Festival), Lajas

**July**
Festival del Mondogo (Tripe Festival), Camuy

**August**
Festival Nacional del Cabro (Goat Festival), Guaynabo

**September**
Festival de la Guayaba (Guava Festival), Aguas Buenas

**October**
Festival del Plátano (Banana Festival), Corozal

**November**
Festival Indígena (Indigenous Festival), Jayuya

**December**
Festival del Petate (Palm Tree Festival), Sabana Grande

# ENJOY CLASSIC PUERTO RICAN HOSPITALITY AT A PARADOR

You won't find big-name hotel brands outside of the island's major cities. Instead, you'll get the chance to discover a unique type of guesthouse that is distinctly Puerto Rican: the parador. These independently owned inns all have fewer than seventy-five rooms, and they embrace the culture and heritage of their regions. In fact, many paradores occupy sites of historic significance, like Hacienda Juanita, a thirty-four-room inn on a former coffee farm high in the mountains of Maricao, or the stately twenty-seven-room Parador Guánica 1929, where travelers have stayed for nearly a century. No two paradores are the same; some feature restaurants, bars, pools, and conference space, while others offer simpler accommodations. But while the amenities and the scenery differ from place to place, you'll always be greeted with a warm welcome.

Hacienda Juanita
Carr. 105 km 22.5, Bo. Afuera, Maricao
787-903-0307
haciendajuanitapr.com

Parador Guánica 1929
Carr. 3116 km 2.5, Bo. Ensenada, Guánica
787-821-0099
tropicalinnspr.com/parador-guanica-1929

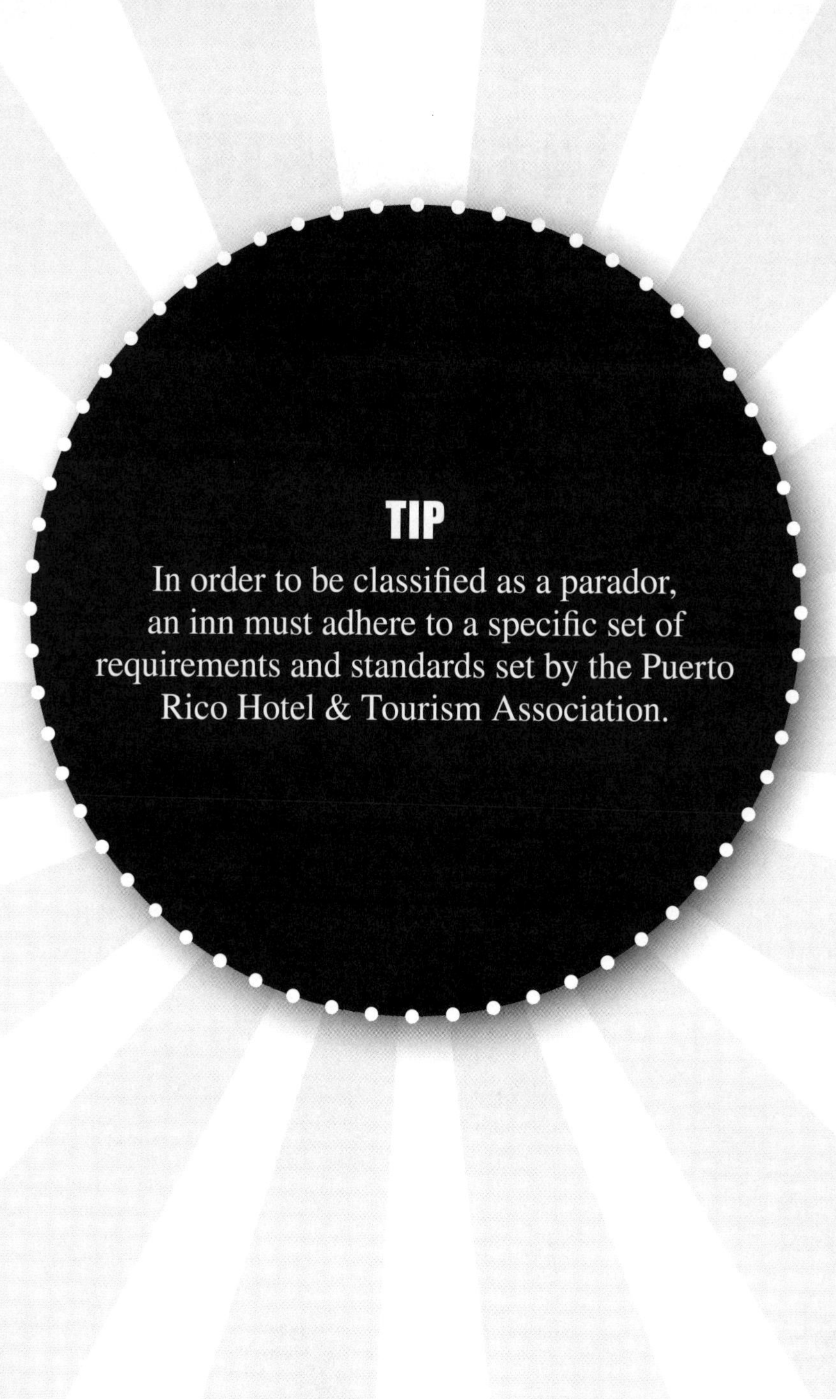
TIP
In order to be classified as a parador, an inn must adhere to a specific set of requirements and standards set by the Puerto Rico Hotel & Tourism Association.

# WALK IN THE FOOTSTEPS OF THE TAÍNOS

## AT CAGUANA INDIGENOUS CEREMONIAL PARK

Before Puerto Rico was Puerto Rico, it was called Borikén, so named by the Taíno Indians who inhabited the islands for centuries. While the Taíno population was nearly decimated after the Spanish arrived, evidence of their beliefs, practices, and culture remain. Centro Ceremonial Indígena de Caguana (Caguana Indigenous Ceremonial Park) in Utuado offers a fascinating glimpse into Taíno life and is considered one of the most important archaeological sites in the Caribbean. Ten ceremonial courts, called bateyes, have been discovered here, which suggests that the area hosted religious rituals, social events, and ball games between the years 1200 and 1500 AD. At this National Historic Landmark, you can walk between the bateyes, touch the petroglyph-etched stones that surround them, and visit a small museum that showcases jewelry, tools, and other excavated relics.

Carr. 111 km 12.3, Bo. Caguana, Utuado
787-894-7325

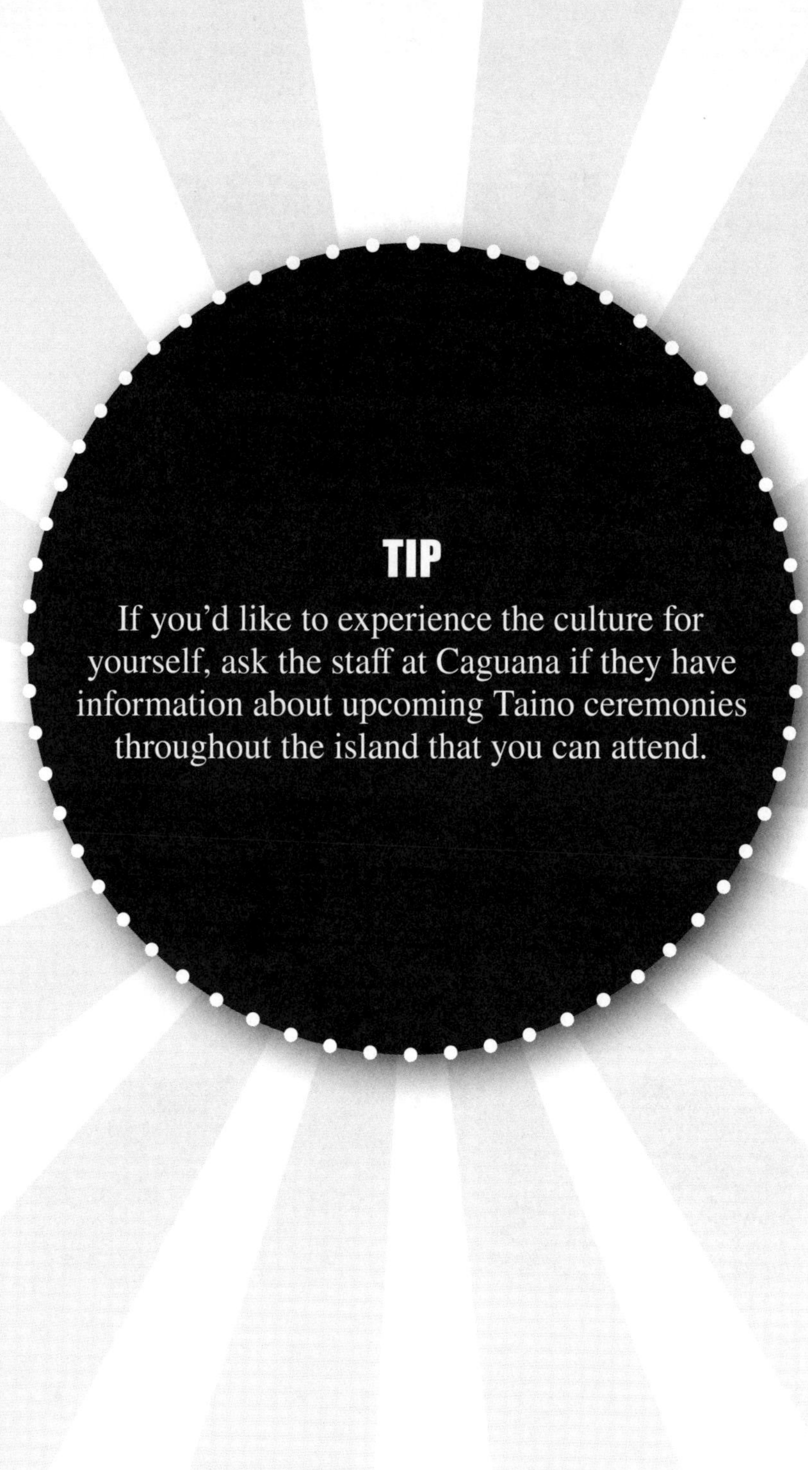

## TIP

If you'd like to experience the culture for yourself, ask the staff at Caguana if they have information about upcoming Taino ceremonies throughout the island that you can attend.

# SEE THE *FLAMING JUNE* AT THE MUSEO DE ARTE DE PONCE

In 1959, Luis A. Ferré, who was later elected governor of Puerto Rico, founded the Museo de Arte de Ponce. Four years later, he purchased what was to become the crown jewel of the museum: Sir Frederic Leighton's *Flaming June*. First unveiled in London in 1895, this Victorian oil painting, often called the *Mona Lisa* of the Caribbean, is an instantly recognizable masterpiece admired by art aficionados around the world. While the iconic image is reason enough to visit, the museum's extensive collection of works by European, Caribbean, and American artists is considered one of the most important in the Americas. The building itself is also a triumph to behold; it was designed by Edward Durrell Stone, the architect responsible for the Museum of Modern Art in New York City and the Kennedy Center in Washington, DC.

2325 Blvd. Luis A. Ferré Aguayo, Ponce
787-840-1510
museoarteponce.org

### TIP

You can join a guided tour every day at 11 a.m. (noon on Sundays) and 2 p.m., except on Tuesdays, when the museum is closed.

# LOOK OUT

## ONTO THE COMERÍO DAM

Towering at 137 feet high, La Represa de Comerío (the Comerío Dam) is impressive to look at even by today's standards, but when it was first built in 1913, it was a major technological feat. Its official name is La Represa El Salto II, and, together with La Represa El Salto I, the dam once provided half of Puerto Rico with power. While it is no longer used to generate electricity, it remains an exciting attraction to see. As you approach from PR-167, you'll hear the sheer force of the water as it spills into the reservoir below. Drive a little farther and you'll come upon an observation deck with shaded benches where you can get a head-on view of the dam in all its glory.

Carr. 167 km 3.2, Bo. Doña Elena, Comerío

### TIP

Next to the lookout point, Restaurante La Barranca is a great spot to rest your legs and grab a bite.

# SALUTE THE MODERN-DAY HEROES
## OF THE PEPINO POWER AUTHORITY

Not every hero wears a cape; some show up in hard hats and yellow vests. Two weeks after Hurricane Maria destroyed Puerto Rico's electrical grid in September 2017, Mayor Javier Jiménez of San Sebastián decided to take action and take care of his people. Instead of waiting for help to arrive, he assembled a group of electricians, public safety personnel, and retired power company workers who became known as the Pepino Power Authority (PPA). Block by block, this grassroots effort ultimately restored electricity for nearly all the city's thirty-seven thousand residents. A permanent exhibit in the Sala Municipal de Exposiciones honors the PPA through a display of photos, letters, tools, and news coverage from around the world. The space is open to visitors Friday through Sunday.

Sala Municipal de Exposiciones
1-7 Calle Luis Muñoz Rivera, San Sebastián

**TIP**

Because of the valiant work of the PPA, Puerto Rican law now allows local governments to create their own power authorities during emergencies.

# GET FIRED UP
## AT PARQUE DE BOMBAS

When you walk through Plaza Las Delicias in the center of Ponce, you can't miss Parque de Bombas, a historic fire station with an eye-catching red and black exterior that makes it one of the most recognizable buildings in Puerto Rico. Originally constructed in 1882 as the main pavilion for the Exposition Fair, the site was repurposed the following year as the headquarters for the island's first-ever fire department. The open-air structure now houses a museum dedicated to firefighters, complete with an original fire engine, photographs, tools, and equipment. While you can explore Parque de Bombas and Plaza Las Delicias on your own, Isla Caribe leads entertaining and educational guided tours loaded with interesting tidbits and historical context.

Parque de Bombas
Plaza Las Delicias, Ponce
visitponce.com/parque-de-bombas

Isla Caribe Tours
939-265-5691
islacaribepr.com

### TIP

Taking a cue from Parque de Bombas, Ponce later adopted red and black as its official colors, which you'll see reflected in its flag, sports teams' uniforms, and other items that represent the city.

91

# CHECK OUT THE VIEWS
## FROM (AND OF) PUERTO RICO'S LIGHTHOUSES

In the nineteenth century, the Spanish broke ground on fifteen lighthouses across the archipelago of Puerto Rico, guiding the way for sailors to make it safely to port. Today, each has evolved into a unique tourist destination, like the small historical museum at Punta Mulas on Vieques or the broken brick remains of Aguadilla's Punta Borinquen Lighthouse, which was destroyed in a tsunami in 1918. The shell of the long-abandoned Guánica Lighthouse is overgrown with plants and covered in colorful graffiti, while kids love the pirate-themed playground, water park, and petting zoo at Arecibo Lighthouse Park. Adding these attractions—which are spread across seven islands—to your to-do list is a fun, scenic way to get to know Puerto Rico.

**TIP**

After the Spanish-American War, the United States built a sixteenth lighthouse on Isla de Cabras (Cabras Island) off the coast of Ceiba.

Arecibo Lighthouse and Historical Park (Arecibo)

Cabezas de San Juan Lighthouse (Fajardo)

Cabras Lighthouse (Ceiba)

Caja de Muertos Lighthouse (Ponce)

Cardona Island Lighthouse (Ponce)

Culebrita Island Lighthouse (Culebra)

El Morro (San Juan)

Guánica Lighthouse (Guánica)

Los Morrillos Lighthouse (Cabo Rojo)

Mona Lighthouse (Mona Island/Mayagüez)

Punta Borinquen Lighthouse (Aguadilla)

Punta de las Figuras (Arroyo)

Punta Higuero Lighthouse (Rincon)

Punta Mulas Lighthouse (Vieques)

Puerto Ferro Lighthouse (Vieques)

Punta Tuna Lighthouse (Maunabo)

# WATCH THE TURBINES SPIN

## AT SANTA ISABEL WIND FARM

As you approach Finca de Viento Santa Isabel (Santa Isabel Wind Farm) from Highway 53, dozens of spinning turbines seem to rise from the area's flat surroundings, fanning out into the distance on either side of the road. Run by Pattern Energy, this 5,500-acre complex is the largest wind energy facility in the Caribbean and a leader in sustainable energy production. The work done here conserves more than ninety-three million gallons of water each year and offsets the carbon dioxide emissions of the equivalent of thirty-five thousand cars. In total, forty-four turbines generate enough renewable energy annually to power thirty thousand homes and businesses. While the farm isn't open to the public, from afar it offers one of the most enchanting vistas on the island.

Carr. 153 km 2.4, Bo. Paso Seco
Santa Isabel
787-971-0030
patternenergy.com/learn/portfolio/santa-isabel-wind

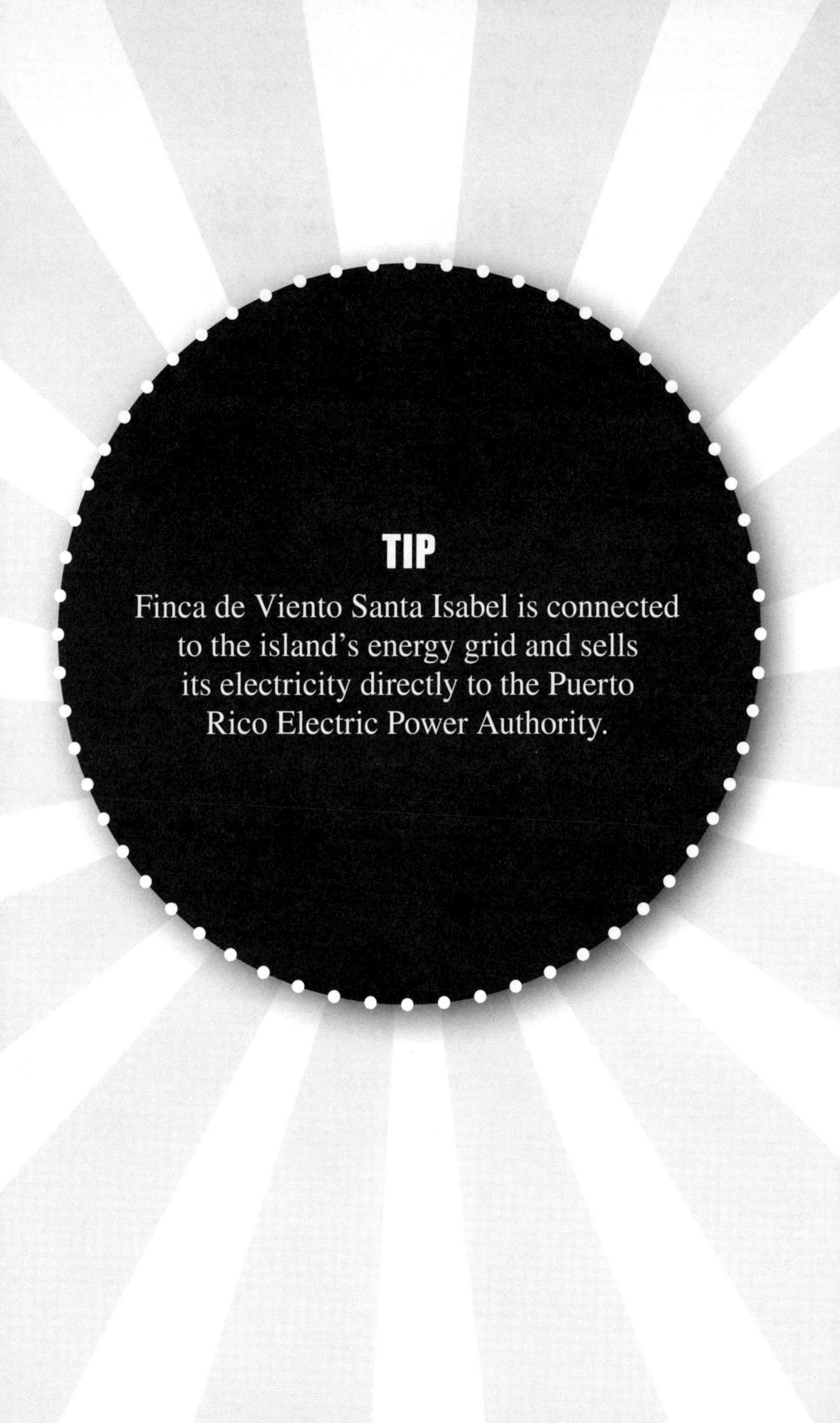

## TIP

Finca de Viento Santa Isabel is connected to the island's energy grid and sells its electricity directly to the Puerto Rico Electric Power Authority.

# EXPERIENCE THE EPITOME OF BESPOKE SERVICE
## AT MONT CARPE DIEM

At Mont Carpe Diem, a boutique inn set high in the hills of Bayamón, each stay is an opportunity to disconnect from the screens in front of you and reconnect with the world around you. Your experience begins when owner Yohandra Toranzo welcomes you with a mojito made with muddled mint from her herb garden. From there, nearly every aspect of your stay is customized, from the music playing in your room to the temperature of your bottled water to the fresh-picked ingredients in your farm-to-table meals. With just two guest cabins, the sixteen-acre property feels at once exclusive and inviting. You can indulge in a massage under a canopy of trees, watch peacocks strut the grounds, swim in the saltwater pool, and fall asleep to the calls of the coquí frogs.

Carr. 879 km 2.5, Bo. X100, Bayamón
787-539-4848
montcarpediem.com

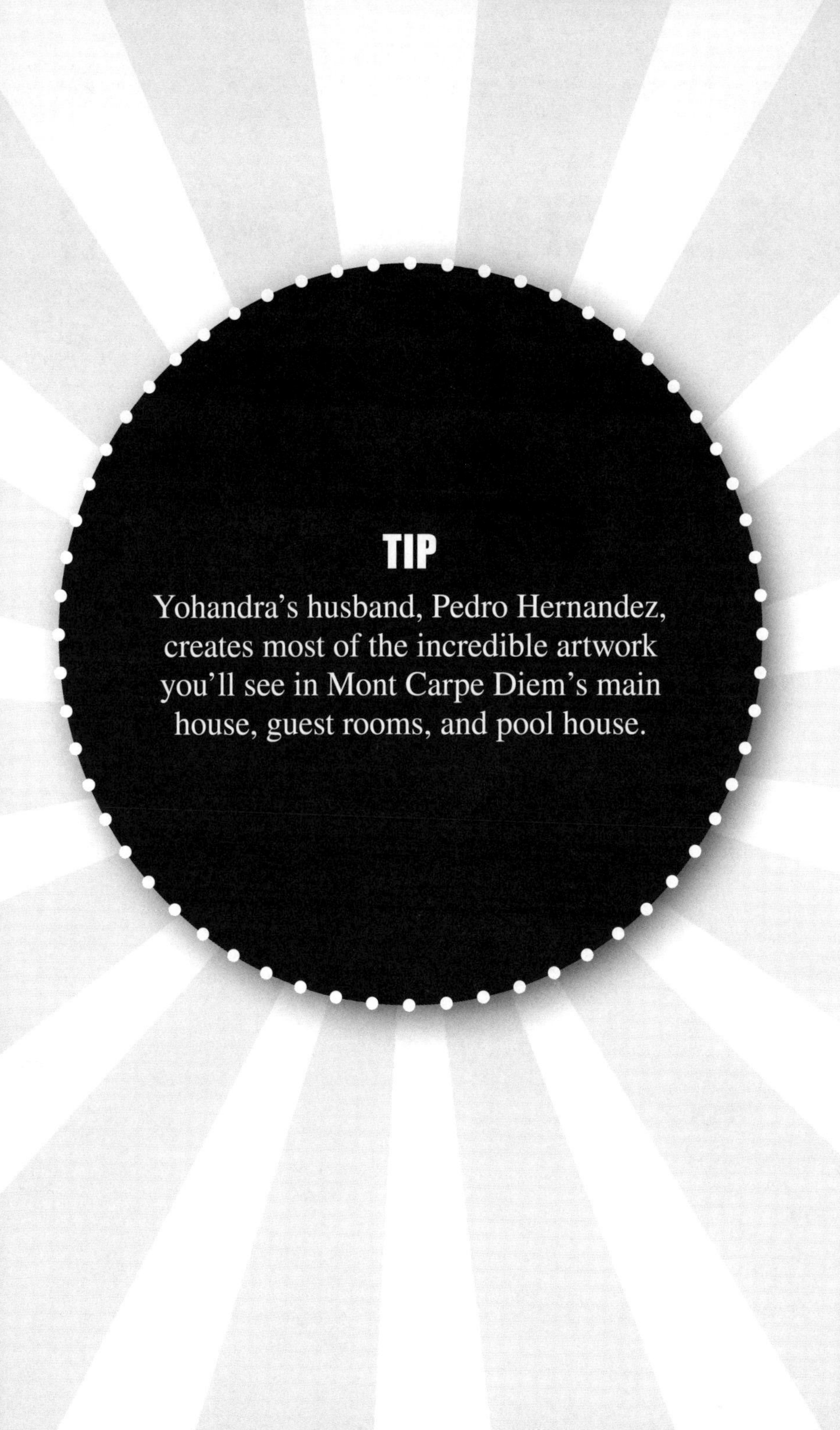

## TIP

Yohandra's husband, Pedro Hernandez, creates most of the incredible artwork you'll see in Mont Carpe Diem's main house, guest rooms, and pool house.

94

# SEE A CENTURY'S WORTH OF MACHETES
## AT HACIENDA LA ESPERANZA

At the height of Puerto Rico's sugar boom in the nineteenth century, Hacienda La Esperanza in Manatí was one of the most important plantations on the island. Today, you can explore the 2,312-acre site at your leisure or on a guided tour that highlights the area's natural resources and its historical value. Its close proximity to the Río Grande de Manatí, which provided nutrient-rich soil for the farm, creates a protected ecosystem that supports a variety of local wildlife and vegetation. You'll also find several historically significant items in the rebuilt manor house, like an embroidered cloth that freed slaves used to voice their grievances and a collection of 389 different styles of machetes made between 1870 and 1970.

Carr. 616 km 6.5, Bo. Cantito, Manatí
787-722-5882
paralanaturaleza.org/en/hacienda-la-esperanza

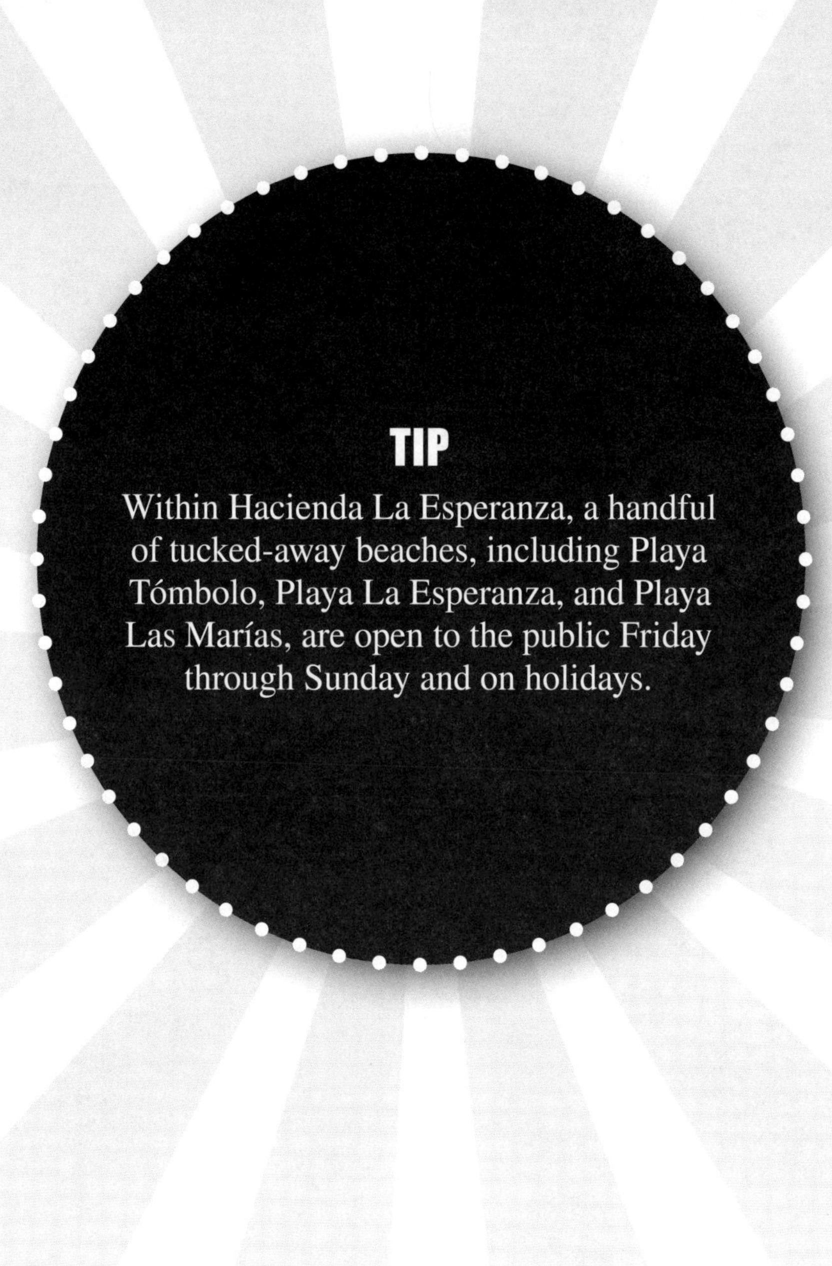
TIP
Within Hacienda La Esperanza, a handful of tucked-away beaches, including Playa Tómbolo, Playa La Esperanza, and Playa Las Marías, are open to the public Friday through Sunday and on holidays.

Olé, Old San Juan
(Photo Credit: Allan Jeffs)

# SHOPPING AND FASHION

95

# SUPPORT LOCAL ARTISTS AND ARTISANS

## AT THE RINCÓN ART WALK

Thursday nights in Rincón mean one thing: Art Walk, a weekly marketplace that celebrates creativity and community. Dozens of local vendors fill the Plaza de Recreo selling handmade items like colorful paintings, carved wood home décor, sparkly jewelry, locally sourced honey, and all-natural soaps. Interacting with the artisans and artists makes each purchase even more special. The multifaceted event also features bands playing live tunes while guests of all ages dance and sing along, as well as food stands selling sweets like chocolate and baked goods. Hungry for more? You'll find everything from Spanish tapas to house-made pasta to shepherd's pie at the modern restaurants that surround the plaza.

Carr. 115, Rincón Pueblo, Rincón

**TIP**

Bring cash.
Many of the market's vendors don't accept credit cards.

96

# BUY A CUSTOM-MADE HAT
## AT OLÉ

When in Puerto Rico, wear a Panama hat. With its wide brim and lightweight, thatched-palm shell, this timeless staple of every Caribbean wardrobe offers the perfect mix of style and sun protection. Savvy shoppers buy theirs at Olé in Old San Juan, where owner Guillermo Christian Jeffs has been peddling custom-fit Panama hats—and only Panama hats—at his hole-in-the-wall shop since the 1970s. The store gets its supply from Ecuador where, contrary to what the name implies, all authentic Panama hats originate. Choose the style and color you like, pick out a ribbon, and let Guillermo and his daughter, Ingrid, do the rest. They'll find the right size, mold it to fit your head, and within minutes, you'll walk out with your new favorite accessory.

105 Calle Fortaleza, Old San Juan
787-724-2445
olepuertorico.com

**TIP**

To keep your hat looking sharp for years to come, grab a flyer with instructions on how to take care of it at home.

# FIND ANYTHING AND EVERYTHING
## AT THE SAN SEBASTIÁN MARKET

Every Friday for more than fifty years, buyers and sellers from all over Puerto Rico have come together at the San Sebastián Market. Starting at 8 a.m., the open-air plaza is packed with more than two hundred vendors peddling, well, everything. Browse handmade jewelry and hammocks. Stock up on Mallorca rolls and motor oil. Pick up a lawn ornament or a light switch or even a live bird. Bring home succulents and spices and salted cod and … you get the idea. If you can think of it, you can probably buy it here. But more than just a place to shop, this weekly bazaar is a cultural phenomenon that you have to experience in person to fully appreciate.

Carr. 125 km 20.2, Bo. Bahomamey, San Sebastián
787-896-3210
facebook.com/plaza.comerciantes

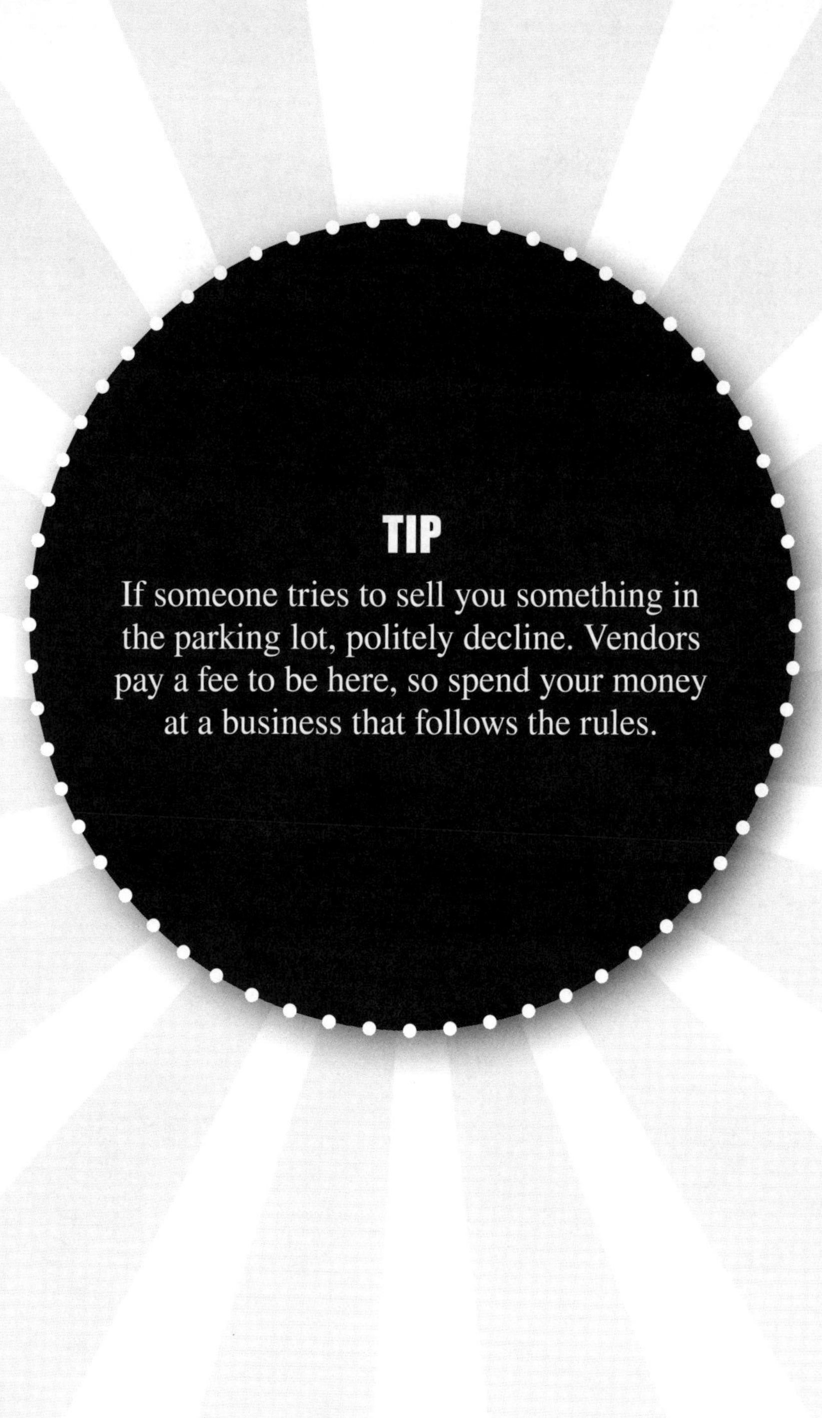
TIP
If someone tries to sell you something in the parking lot, politely decline. Vendors pay a fee to be here, so spend your money at a business that follows the rules.

98

# SHOP FOR ALL THINGS BOTANICAL IN AIBONITO

Whether you make your living in landscaping, love getting your hands dirty in your home garden, or simply can't get enough of fresh flowers and plants, Aibonito is the place for you. Known as Puerto Rico's Garden, this bucolic municipality in the mountains of central Puerto Rico is a horticultural heaven where you can buy everything from delicate orchids to sapling fruit trees to medicinal succulents. And if you're in the market for accessories like planters, gardening tools, and lawn ornaments, you'll find those, too. The most exciting time to make the trip is during the annual Festival de las Flores (Flower Festival) each summer, when thousands of locals and visitors descend on Aibonito to enjoy more than a week of exhibits, marketplaces, live music, and celebrations.

Aibonito Flower Route
rutas.aibonitopr.net/listing-category/ruta-flores

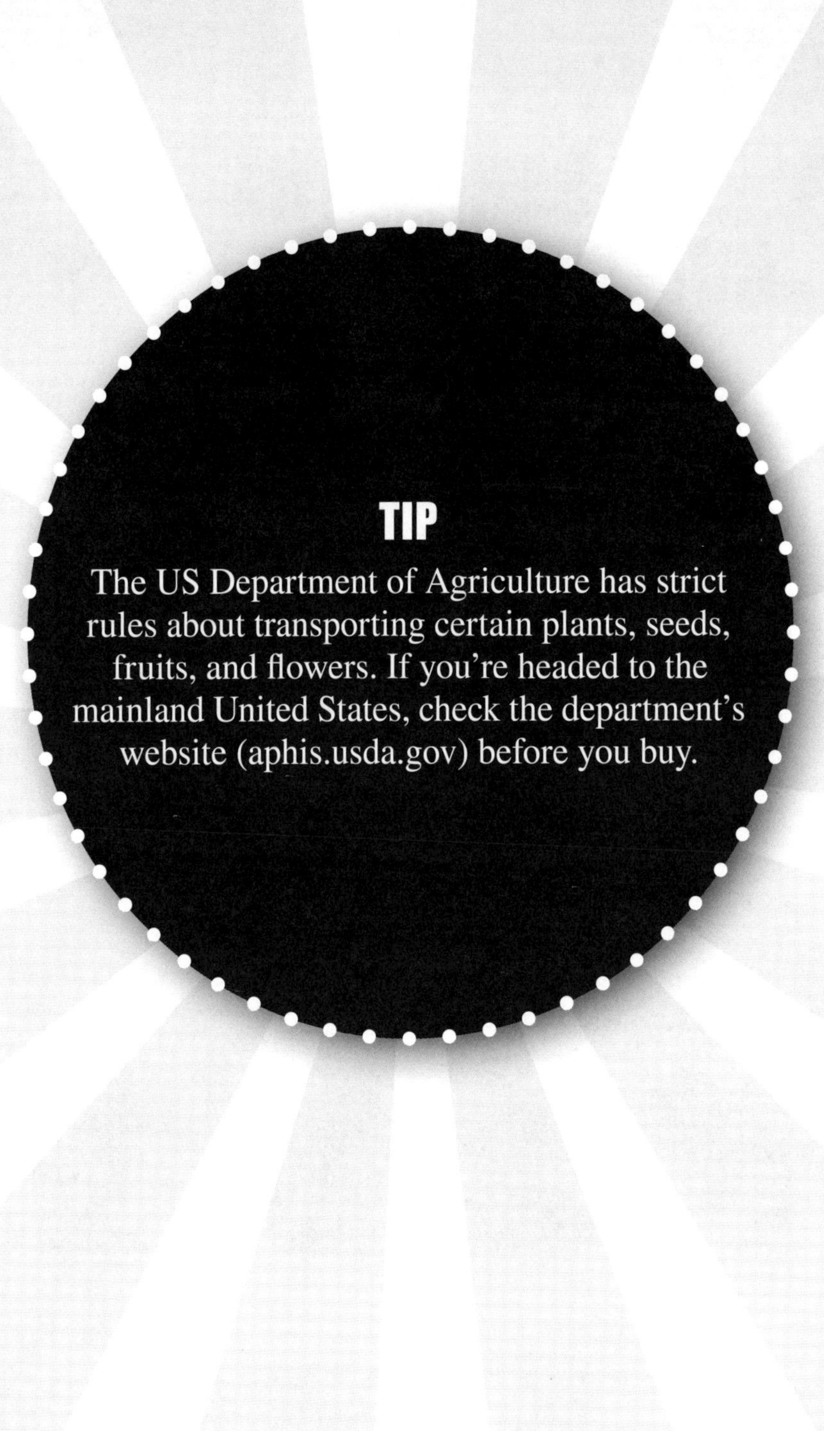

## TIP

The US Department of Agriculture has strict rules about transporting certain plants, seeds, fruits, and flowers. If you're headed to the mainland United States, check the department's website (aphis.usda.gov) before you buy.

# STROLL THE COBBLESTONE STREETS
## OF OLD SAN JUAN

With centuries-old architecture, important cultural sites, and eclectic boutiques, Old San Juan blends historic charm with a modern, metropolitan vibe. Give yourself at least a day to wander through the narrow cobblestone streets and take in the sights, sounds, and energy of the city. Stop into one-of-a-kind shops like The Butterfly People, a showroom for Lucite-encased butterfly art, and Concalma, which sells handbags manufactured at an industrial women's co-op in Utuado. Explore attractions like the Museo de Las Américas and Catedral San Juan Bautista. Feed the pigeons at Parque de las Palomas. And when hunger strikes, head to Calle Recinto Sur, a strip of Puerto Rican and international restaurants, most of which offer outdoor seating with superb people watching.

**TIP**

For guided experiences that focus on different aspects of the city, like history, culture, and gastronomy, book an excursion with operators including Spoon Food Tours or Tour Old San Juan.

**The Butterfly People**
257 Calle De La Cruz, Old San Juan
787-723-2432
butterflypeople.com

**Concalma**
207 Calle San Francisco, Old San Juan
787-342-9757
shopconcalma.com

**Museo de las Américas**
Cuartel de Ballajá, 2nd floor, Old San Juan
787-724-5052
museolasamericas.org

**Parque de las Palomas**
Calle de Tetuán, Old San Juan

100

# BROWSE THE BOUTIQUES
## ON CALLE LOÍZA

With vibrant street art, colorful characters, and a rough-around-the-edges vibe, Santurce easily claims the title of San Juan's coolest neighborhood. In the past few years, the run-down stretch of Calle Loíza has emerged as a harbinger of hip, as empty storefronts have given way to a handful of trendy boutiques where you can spend the day browsing and buying. Stop into spots like Nude and T Playa for a stylish selection of bathing suits, beachwear, and accessories. Much like the area itself, Len.T.juela melds old and new, stocking the racks with a mix of vintage pieces and lines from up-and-coming designers. And you never know what local artists might pop in to showcase their work amidst the fashion-forward apparel at Moni & Coli.

### TIP

Loíza Street also boasts a string of buzzy eateries. Snack on artisan desserts at Double Cake, order a juicy burger at Dude's Diner, or show up early to snag a seat for Sunday brunch at the uber-popular Sabrina.

**Nude**
1750 Calle Loíza, Bo. Santurce, San Juan
787-728-7074
shopnude.com

**T Playa**
1804 Calle Loíza, Bo. Santurce, San Juan
facebook.com/tplayasj

**Len.T.juela**
1852 Calle Loíza, Bo. Santurce, San Juan
787-408-7111
shoplentejuela.com

**Moni & Coli**
1762 Calle Loíza, Bo. Santurce, San Juan
787-727-6839
moniandcoli.com

Surfing in Rincón
(Photo Credit: racheltannerphotography.com)

# SUGGESTED ITINERARIES

## OUTDOOR ADVENTURE



## ANIMAL LOVERS

## GREAT FOR KIDS



## BEACH BUMS



## ART FANS

## RAINY DAYS

El Poblado, Boquerón
(Photo Credit: Amy Gordon)

# ACTIVITIES BY REGION

## OLD SAN JUAN



## SAN JUAN METRO AREA

## NORTHERN COAST



## SOUTHWEST



## CORDILLERA CENTRAL MOUNTAINS

## EAST COAST, VIEQUES, AND CULEBRA

# INDEX